There's a Hole in the Sky

Tracking Down God
in the Company of
the De-Churched

TERRY GILES

**There's a Hole in the Sky: Tracking Down God
in the Company of the De-Churched**
Copyright © 2011 Terry Giles

ISBN: 1456527363
ISBN-13: 9781456527365
Library of Congress Control Number: 2011900361

Cover art by William J. Doan.

For Cheryl

Contents

There's a Hole in the Sky

I suspect that no matter how hard we try, none of us can really escape the religion of our childhood. One of my earliest memories is of a picture hung on a cement block wall in the musty smelling basement of a small white church. The picture was a painting of God surrounded by beams of golden light and gazing down upon a small group of little children playing in a green meadow spotted with wildflowers. God was looking at us through a hole in the sky. Upstairs in the "big people's church" I heard singing about clouds rolling back and I even heard the preacher say that someday the skies would part and Jesus would reappear. I can remember lying on my back more than once, surrounded by the tall grass in the field across the dirt road next to our house, intently studying the clouds to see if I could find that hole. I knew it must be there. And if a peal of thunder unexpectedly rang out (or a passing truck backfired), my expectation grew. Try as I might, though, I never did find that hole in the sky.

A lot has happened since I first saw that painting of God looking through a hole in the sky. Although I no longer look upward to see if the clouds are fleeing away from each other, I'm more certain than ever that the hole is there, and I guess I'm still looking for it. Truth be told, I think we all are. Not a literal rearrangement of the clouds that might show up on a Doppler radar, but we are all looking for that means of access, that connection, whereby we might know the Divine. That is what this book is about—a hole in the sky.

THE NERVE OF SUCH A THING!

I can think of few things cheekier than a book on God. On one level, the idea itself seems to me utterly absurd. How could any of us ever hope to capture the essence of the Divine, let alone claim to have found the right words by which to describe God! Only the most foolhardy or the most blindly arrogant would ever travel that road. Fortunately, I've usually (but not always) managed to avoid both extremes of arrogance and foolhardiness, so I will make far more modest claims in the pages you are about to read. This book is not an attempt to define God.

This book is about getting to know God. Consequently, what you are about to read concerns us—you and me, those who would like to know God—every bit as much as it concerns God. Certainly, during the course of our exploration together, we will think aloud about some of the characteristics of God, investigate something of the Divine's personality, and look at some of the more remarkable things the Divine has done. But in all this there will be no pretense of having defined, categorized, or in any other conceivable fashion pronounced the final word on God. It just can't be done. A little later on I'll explain why. But this caveat doesn't mean we are left hopelessly lost in our quest to know God or that there isn't a God to know. All my admission really means is that the quest will have no end. We will never have arrived. We will never be experts. And we will always need to be open to divine surprises. In light of all this, my hope is that we can share the various paths we have walked on our journey in knowing God, and the glimpses of God we've been afforded along the way.

A THEOLOGY FOR THE NONRELIGIOUS

Given the qualifiers I've felt compelled to make in the last several paragraphs, the obvious question arises: Why bother? What makes this book any different from the dozens of other religious self-helps, "secrets" to knowing God, or even highbrow academic-sounding books on God and the spiritual life?

Perhaps it sounds confused and contradictory, but if I could have my wish, the book you now hold would best be described as a theology for nonreligious people. But hold on; give me just a minute more. I know that for many people "theology" is a dirty word—or at least a cue to begin yawning, followed by a distant and glazed look in the eye. So let me explain my wish.

There is a growing rift between religion and spirituality, an observation supported by several recent and comprehensive national surveys that we'll look at later. Many people, intent on developing intimacy with God, have not found much help in religious forms currently in vogue. Formal religious affiliation is declining, yet interest in spirituality is on the rise. This means that, more and more, questions about spirituality are left unanswered by religious offerings. It's the people who feel this tension between religion and spirituality, who have little or no interest in religion, for whom the following pages were written.

A BOOK FOR THE DE-CHURCHED

I recently finished an email exchange with a young woman who powerfully expressed a vibrant spirituality despite her distrust of religion. She is building a life and a career working in nonprofit organizations. She wrote,

> My career is the best way I know how to serve God. I don't feel that I have a choice. I feel that if I didn't work for social justice I would cease to exist. Logically, that doesn't make sense, but I guess I feel like I was created to do what I'm doing. I've always thought that's what it means to be "called

by God" to a task. I'm not passionate about justice because I believe that everyone deserves the help I give them, I'm passionate about social justice because every fiber of my being says it's right and good to live this way and to see the world this way. For me, to see it a different way would mean being separate from God, from my family, from nature, and from myself. It would mean losing the intelligence, creativity, imagination, laughter, and other qualities that make us human....

... I have found that a majority of the people I meet around my age have a strong desire to be part of a faith community but are repulsed by traditional churches. I think the rise of NGOs [nongovernmental organizations] is also a reflection of people turning away from churches and creating different communities.

If you resonate with the lines of this email, this book is for you.

Quite often, theology for nonreligious people takes the form of a creative novel or fictional tale intent on inspiring the reader by weaving an underlying set of ideas into the plot of the story. Some of these books are very compelling and have plugged in to the currently favored perception that "truth" is best seen in the concrete, lived-out experience rather than the abstract or dogmatic assemblage of ideas only. But if you are like me, you frequently come away from a book like that thinking, "Yeah, it looks good in the realm of story and contrived fiction, but what about in real life? Is it true?" Creative imagination can be helpful—it can provide new perspectives, new ways of looking at life—but in the end the question "Is it true?" persists. In the pages that follow, that one little question will nag us constantly. We will consider some big ideas and we'll look at some stories to illustrate those ideas and make them concrete. But since these stories come from real life, some end well but many do not. Regardless, our goal will always be to find the answer to the one little question: Is it true?

A Disclaimer or Two

Before we begin our travels together, permit me a word or two of further explanation. As you venture further into this book, you will quickly discover that I am heavily indebted to the Bible. The Bible has been a welcome partner on my journey. It contains invaluable ideas and viewpoints. Perhaps you have found similar help in other sacred books or in other sources altogether. My silence concerning those other books or sources should not be interpreted as a suggestion that I see no value in those other books and sources. It's just that they have not been part of my journey to the same extent as the Bible. Even though I make no apology for my indebtedness to the Bible—the Bible has made a tremendous impact on me—I do not assume that you, either now or in the future, will share my enthusiasm. In fact, I suspect you may not identify with any religious group or church, and the Bible, more than likely, is a closed book to you. Chances are you may belong to that fast growing "de-churched" population. In a later chapter we will think together about some of the problems inherent in a religious knowledge of God, but for now let me simply tell you I welcome your partnership regardless of your religious affiliation or non-affiliation. You need not adhere to a particular religious creed or custom in order to engage with this book. It isn't my goal to convert you.

PLAN OF THE BOOK

This book is written in four parts. Part 1 considers two very formidable problems we must engage in our quest to know God. In these pages, we examine the role religion plays (or does not play) in forming our knowledge of God, as well as the difficulty represented by the very real and inescapable horrors experienced in the world around us. If there is a God to know, the questions raised in this part of the book must be answered. In Part 2 we give our attention to the nuts and bolts of how we can know God. In this section, we will establish three guiding questions by which we can test the validity of our knowledge of God. Those questions will help us evaluate all that follows. Part 3 is devoted to a three-part description of God, a description that happens to dominate the pages of the Bible but also is core to the way most people think and talk about God. In some ways, this description of God in Part 3 forms the heart of the book. The last part of this book, Part 4, looks at two flesh-and-blood, life-changing "so whats" of our search for a hole in the sky. If there is anything at all to this business of knowing God, those engaged in the quest will find themselves forever changed. In Part 4, we consider two of those changes.

WE'RE NOT CALLING THE SHOTS

My own search for a hole in the sky has led me to unexpected, unplanned, and at times unwanted experiences and places. The sometimes lonely and inexpressibly dark trails contained in my quest have literally taken me all over the world and put me in situations I could not have dreamed. But these dark and terrible paths have been more than matched by encounters and tracks that have left me breathless and awestruck. It has occurred to me, much too late, that in my search for a hole in the sky,

I have not been in control. I have not dictated or directed the circumstances, time, place, or outcome of my search. Someone else has been calling the shots. I now understand that my search has, in reality, been a partnership with an Unseen Companion who has been on this quest before. I mention this here because I suspect that as you continue this search for a hole in the sky, you too may find yourself not in charge. It's a risk, make no mistake. But it's a risk worth the taking. So before we begin, count the cost. Surprises may be in store for you, and neither you nor I can predict where our journey will take you on your search for a hole in the sky.

Excursus 1
God: He and She

As you read this book, you will notice before not too many pages that I usually refer to God by using the masculine pronouns "he" or "him." That usage needs an explanation and perhaps an apology. I am not foolish enough to think God is masculine, or that masculine gender connotations are somehow better suited to God. So on one level, I admit my usage is partly a result of convenience and habit. I grew up using this kind of terminology for God, and it just seems right to me. Yet, I am very aware that words are important, and my convenience is a poor excuse for perpetrating an inaccuracy should my use of the masculine suggest a limitation or inappropriate way of referring to Deity. To those who find a gendered reference to God a roadblock, I apologize. I mean no offense, and I certainly do not wish to imply that God is offended by a feminine label. If so, the writer of the biblical book of Hosea is in deep, deep trouble! That writer understood quite well—better than I do—the beauty, strength, and wealth of meaning communicated by feminine references to God. Right in the middle of an overwhelmingly masculine presentation of God, Hosea uses a decidedly feminine description, likening God to a loving mother teaching a toddler to walk (Hosea 11:3).This mention of Hosea leads me to a partial explanation of why I refer to God as he. Hosea is clear evidence (and he is not alone[1]) that the biblical writers were not so enmeshed in a patriarchal society that they became blind to the possibilities and even the necessity of referring to God as she. They were quite able to choose the masculine *or* the feminine when referring to God, and generally they chose the masculine. There were a variety of reasons for their choices, some of which still seem valid to me.

For those Bible writers, the use of masculine and feminine signified a certain and generally identifiable social place within a network of social relationships. Father communicated something different than Mother. The same with brother/sister; king/queen; god/goddess. Each of these words communicates a network of social interrelationships that go beyond the gender of the individual upon whom the label is placed. The list could go on and on. For us, those gender-defined social places are changing, and the gender-specific pronouns, when applied to God, no longer work the same way they did for many of the biblical authors. The easiest example and, in my estimation, one of the most painful is the meanings progressively attached to the word *father.* For far too many of us, "father" brings to mind absent or abusive. Or, if we think television sitcoms

---

1   Isaiah 49:15 is another example.

an accurate reflection of public sentiment, "father" means a bumbling and self-centered incompetent. The biblical writers had a far different picture in mind when using "father" in reference to God. So, if we want to recapture the image of God they intended, we may well need to rescue the word, swimming against the cultural current, or find a different word that now communicates the social realities intended by the biblical writers when referring to God in this way. All too often, linguistic rescue is out of the question as impractical and ineffective, leaving us no alternative but to search for new terminology.

All this being the case, is there any excuse to still use "he" or "him" in reference to God? Yes, I believe so. First, the very fact that biblical writers use both genders in reference to God means they use each gendered reference for a reason, fully aware of the differences and limitations of each in their own culture. The masculine communicates certain emphasis and the feminine communicates other emphasis. To refuse to use either the masculine or the feminine risks losing the distinctive contribution made by both the masculine and the feminine. Because I respect and value the feminine references to God, I will continue to use the masculine in instances I believe appropriate. I will also use feminine references when those are more appropriate. A second reason I still use the masculine in reference to God is that as honestly and as clearly as I can discern, that usage is authentic to my own journey—to this point at least. So, even though I have attempted to be quite intentional in my usage of pronouns in reference to God, if I offend some of you, I ask your forgiveness and God's (both his and hers).

PART 1
HOUSTON, WE'VE
HAD A PROBLEM

"Houston, we've had a problem." Ever since these words were first uttered by astronaut Jack Swigert, they've functioned as shorthand for the lore surrounding the Apollo 13 moon mission—its hope, desperation, and fear. For many, the search for a hole in the sky is threatened by difficulties that produce the same hope, desperation, and fear as that felt by three astronauts hurtling toward the unknown. In this part of the book we will work our way through two issues that have caused many of us to send our own message into the void: Houston, we've had a problem.

1

God Bites and Religion Sucks: The Problem of Religion in Knowing God

If we are to find a hole in the sky, one of the inescapable concerns we must confront is the sometimes questionable relationship between religion and God. The matter becomes complicated because the relationship is dynamic, a moving target that changes from generation to generation. Right now, the shifting relationship between religion and God is, in many sectors, assuming seismic proportions.

One of the exciting things about teaching college students for a living is that I get to spend time around young adults who are learning to think for themselves, speak their minds, and are in the process of discovering a big and broad universe. Sometimes, they have a tremendous ability to get right to the point without mixing words or caution. I'll never forget one class in which a student related to the rest of us some horrific things she was experiencing right then. A devastating illness, a car accident, and interrupted school financing had all hit her within the space of a few days. She finished her story and the room went silent. You could actually feel the empathy as other students considered what she said and willingly shared her burden. After a few seconds the hush was suddenly interrupted as someone simply replied, "God bites!" For many in that room, those two words went right to the heart of the matter, and the concept is one we must honestly consider if there really is a hole in the sky.

GOD BITES

This pronouncement that "God bites!" isn't made thoughtlessly or without concern. As often as not, a fair amount of passion accompanies the words. The description is generally meant to express utter disappointment in God (the Person), or a total rejection of God (the idea). Often the conclusion that God bites has some substantial evidence behind it, or at least some arguments that are pretty persuasive. Here are a few of them.

I've heard anger directed at God for the way he was used by clerics to justify their actions while raping children. We've all seen God used as decoration for acts of terrorism and war. I've heard him called upon to bring fire down upon "murdering" abortionists and "intolerant, woman-hating" antiabortionists. I've read court records that say God has been used to demand sexual favors by sect leaders, pastors, and spiritual guides. I've listened to sermons in which

God insisted on subservience from women and money from adoring crowds. I hear that God builds pipelines in Alaska, invades Georgia, updates nuclear missiles, and snuffs out the lives of loving parents. From what I've been told, God puts Republicans in office, removes Republicans from office, and hates bridges to nowhere but really loves big church buildings. I've been told that God doesn't mind killing 250,000 Hindus and Muslims in a wall of water surging from the Indian Ocean, but certainly wouldn't do that to Christians. I've even been told that God helped kick a winning field goal in a miraculous come-from-behind football upset. All in all, if what I've been told is true, then I guess I would have to agree: God bites.

AND RELIGION SUCKS!

If God bites, then religion sucks. This opinion, although perhaps not stated so brusquely, is not new and has been expressed in many different ways at many different times. For some in the eighteenth century, God became an outdated and vicious personage best left in the dusty reaches of the distant past along with the traditional religious forms that sought to describe him. Others, in the nineteenth century, concluded that God was a father figure whom humanity had long since outgrown, together with the paternalistic forms of religious authority he seemed to favor. Still others, seeking to free themselves from an imposing and at times despotic deity, confidently pronounced God dead in the middle of the twentieth century, and all forms of religious shackles were thrown off.

For many, it gets very personal. In the years I've been teaching college courses on the Bible or religious studies, I've heard some amazing and at times deeply troubling stories. I will never forget a young woman who approached me after class and just prior to a class trip we were taking to a local church. She was shaking and could hardly contain herself as she told me she was refusing to take part in the class trip. "I really want to take this class," she said, "but there is no way I'm going to that church!" Before I could ask why, she blurted, "I was raped in that church!" And then the floodgates of emotion opened. I wish her story was the only one. I've heard stories of babies denied burial, families broken apart because of sexually preda- tory clergy, molestations, drunken orgies, illicit drug use, unwanted fondling, and misuse of church funds all by local clergy who stand behind pulpits every week and proclaim the love of Jesus. If half of what I've been told is true, then, I must confess, I tend to agree with the generation coming of age in the beginning of the twenty-first century when they simply conclude God bites and religion sucks!

Perhaps you've read the previous two paragraphs and have said to yourself, "Wait a minute. You can't blame God for all the stupid stuff other people try to pin on him. Just because somebody says something about God, that doesn't make it true! And, sure religion has some horrible flaws in it, but it also does a lot of good." And I agree.

It's unfair to paint all religious people and what they think with the same brush. I know some pastors and religious professionals whom I admire very much. They give selflessly to others and are big hearted and kind people. They have helped countless people through periods of loss and transition. I have witnessed in others (and have been on the receiving end myself) the comfort and compassion expressed by God through religious people and professionals. However, I also know some clergy who ought to be in jail and have used their religious positions for crass and undisguised personal gain. In addition, I have seen dramatic changes in personal behavior among people who have been captured by God and are now deeply religious, leading to restored relationships and admirable acts of love and self-sacrifice. But I have also seen people carry large Bibles prominently tucked under their arm while entering a courtroom in an effort to obtain a lighter sentence for a crime committed.

The problem isn't that there are good religious people and bad religious people. The problem is that religion doesn't seem to matter much in making one or the other. Many good people are good without religion and many bad people are bad in spite of their religion. To which a reply could be made: "Sure, but think of how much better those good nonreligious people would be if they only had religion," or "Think of how much worse those bad religious people would be without religion!" This objection doesn't convince me. If God can be known and if religion is the path by which God is known, shouldn't there be evidence of having spent time with God among those who claim such intimacy? Shouldn't something of God have rubbed off among those who say they know him best? Wasn't this what Jesus, himself, was getting at when he commended love for each other as a way outsiders would be certain of religious authenticity (John 17:23; and restated in a manner in 1 John 4:11–14)? So the question must be asked: What role does religion play in knowing God?

To an ever-growing extent, people in the United States are responding to the above question by saying, "Not much!" Given that the fastest-growing religious group in America is the "unaffiliated"[2] (that is, those who claim no religious affiliation in their quest to know God), it's easy to see that the level of discontent with the religious status quo is tracking upward. The rise and growth of the "unaffiliated" shows that apparently there are many people who share a concern and frustration with religion. The sentiments expressed in the opinion "God bites and religion sucks" don't appear to be going away—at least anytime

---

2   According to "U.S. Religious Landscape Survey. Religious Affiliation: Diverse and Dynamic," by the Pew Forum on Religion and Public Life (Washington: Pew Research Center, February 2008). Confirmed by a second recent study: "American Religious Identification Survey" (ARIS 2008), Barry Kosmin and Ariela Keysar (Hartford: Trinity College, 2009).

soon. So if our quest is to know God, how are we to think of the religious part of human experience? Let's see if we can understand *if* and *why* religion matters to those of us seeking to know God.

TOPPLING THE STOOL

Think of it in this fashion. The way we construct knowledge of God, or any religious matter, generally involves one or more of three "knowledge streams": authority, coherence, and experience (we will examine each of these at length in a later chapter). If we think of these as three legs on a "religious knowledge stool," we may have an easier time understanding what lies behind the "unaffiliated" and the frustration currently expressing itself with popular American religion. When one or more legs of this knowledge stool are out of whack or faulty, the whole thing is liable to topple over. That is precisely the condition in which we now find ourselves. The stool of religious knowledge has a serious wobble to it.

Consider one or more of the following scenarios. All too often, religious authorities make statements about God or spiritual realities that are out of sync with the manner in which most of us compose a coherent view of the universe. Generally, the religious statement lacks experiential verifiability, and so dissonance arises as the leg of religious authority is out of balance with the legs of coherence and experience. Here's an example. I recently heard a sermon passionately delivered by a conservative Christian pastor who declared that the universe resulted from a series of divine creative acts occurring in the space of twenty-four hours each and taking place about six thousand years ago. Further, this pastor went on to announce that should this view of origins be rejected, all Christianity—including trust in the redemptive God—becomes suspect and worthless. This *authority* (the pastor's sermon) is at odds with the *coherent* way most people think of the universe and denies the *experience* of trust in the redemptive God those people encounter, even as they disallow a creation spanning only six literal days. The result of pitting this religious authority against a coherent view and experienced trust is a dissonance threatening to topple over the whole stool of religious knowledge, particularly when this one belief is presented as the linchpin for all Christianity.

The stool can be toppled in other ways too. If an experience "shakes your world," calling into question the coherent view of life you have constructed, the religious knowledge stool can easily fall with devastating consequences. An unexpected tragedy or illness, a natural catastrophe, or a war that calls into question a cherished and thought-to-be-rock-solid aspect of the character of God can easily be the occasion for the stool to wobble. Or, if an authority figure acts in a manner inconsistent with the message he or she proclaims (clergy sex scandal, tax-evading televangelist), the experience will, as often as not, conclude with the message being thrown out with the messenger. Once again, the stool of religious knowledge threatens collapse. If this sort of thing happens often enough to enough people (as is true in North America at the beginning of the twenty-first century) it is quite understandable that many of us conclude: religion sucks.

CHANGES ARE ON THE WAY!

Caught midair and trying to stay upright on this wobbly stool, it's easy for us to think this dilemma concerning the trustworthiness of God and religion is brand new and that no one else has ever felt the tensions that accompany religious doubt. But, truth be told, this sort of thing has happened before, and, frankly, a wobbly stool—though at times mighty uncomfortable—isn't always a bad thing when it comes to religion. In fact, it's healthy, now and then, to reconsider the structure of this religious knowledge stool upon which each of us perch.

There is nothing new about changes in religion. But because religious changes involve elements of deep belief, those changes will often involve accusations, charges, and countercharges invoking nothing less than eternal damnation and God's perpetual wrath! Change has happened before and the charge of "heretic" has been weathered by many good people. If you think religion sucks, consider what some other people have said concerning the religious forms of their day:

> Obviously, even if there is no other proof, no one in his right mind will hope for anything good from such an ill-patched hodgepodge. (John Calvin, *Institutes of the Christian Religion*, Book IV.10.11)

> It were needful indeed now to burn the Pope, that is, the Roman papacy together with his teaching and cruelty.... For the kingdom of the Pope is so contrary to the kingdom of Christ and to Christian life that it would be better and safer to live all alone in a desert than to live in the kingdom of the Antichrist. (Martin Luther, "Lectures on Psalms," *The Reformation: A Narrative History Related by Contemporary Observers and Participants*, ed. Hans Hillerbrand [Grand Rapids, MI: Eerdmans, 1964], 86.)

> From these two convictions—that they do not know him and that they persecute and slay his advocates—Christ now passes the judgment that the so-called Church is not

the Church. (Martin Luther, *The Sermons of Martin Luther*, vol. 2, [Grand Rapids, MI: Baker, 1983], 270.)

Consequently we command you, each and all, under the penalties already prescribed, that henceforth no one shall dare to buy, sell, read, preserve, copy, print, or cause to be copied or printed, any books of the aforesaid Martin Luther, condemned by our holy father the Pope as aforesaid, or any other writings in German or Latin hitherto composed by him, since they are foul, harmful, suspected, and published by a notorious and stiffnecked [sic] heretic. (Emperor Charles V, *The Reformation: A Narrative History Related by Contemporary Observers and Participants*, ed. Hans Hillerbrand [Grand Rapids, MI: Eerdmans, 1964], 100.)

…we shall be traduced [slandered] by Popish Persons [Roman Catholics] at home or abroad, who therefore will malign us, because we are poor instruments to make God's holy Truth to be yet more and more known unto the people, whom they desire still to keep in ignorance and darkness; or

if, on the other side, we shall be maligned
by selfconceited [sic] Brethren [Anabaptists],
who run their own ways, and give liking unto
nothing, but what is framed by themselves,
and hammered on their anvil. (Translators'
"Epistle Dedicatory," King James Version)

"Let them alone; they are blind guides of the
blind. And if one blind person guides another,
both will fall into a pit." But Peter said to him,
"Explain this parable to us." Then he said,
"Are you also still without understanding?
Do you not see that whatever goes into the
mouth enters the stomach, and goes out
into the sewer? But what comes out of the
mouth proceeds from the heart, and this
is what defiles. For out of the heart come
evil intentions, murder, adultery, fornication,
theft, false witness, slander. These are what
defile a person, but to eat with unwashed
hands does not defile." (Jesus, Matthew
15:14–20 NRSV)

Hear the word of the LORD, you rulers of
Sodom! Listen to the teaching of our God,
you people of Gomorrah! What to me is the
multitude of your sacrifices? says the LORD; I

have had enough of burnt offerings of rams and the fat of fed beasts; I do not delight in the blood of bulls, or of lambs, or of goats. When you come to appear before me, who asked this from your hand? Trample my courts no more; bringing offerings is futile; incense is an abomination to me. New moon and sabbath and calling of convocation—I cannot endure solemn assemblies with iniquity. Your new moons and your appointed festivals my soul hates; they have become a burden to me, I am weary of bearing them. When you stretch out your hands, I will hide my eyes from you; even though you make many prayers, I will not listen; your hands are full of blood. (God, Isaiah 1:10–15 NRSV)

So here we have it. Church leaders, founders of reform and revival, translators of the most influential English translation of the Bible, Jesus, and God, himself, have all gone on record to say religion sucks! The strong statements voiced above were all particularly powerful, for they were made in protest of what the speaker perceived to be a perversion of good and helpful religious forms. The speaker's recognition that religion can have an important and valid role to play gave urgency to the complaint.

THREE COLLIDING VECTORS OF CHANGE

The same sort of complaint about religion that we just saw from others is going on today. And since, for most of us, our quest to know God is impacted by the way we think about religion, we need to consider the face of religion in America at the beginning of the twenty-first century. In what follows we will not look at particular beliefs or practices held by this or that religious group, but we will take a much broader view, focusing on religious trends. Currently, there are three vectors colliding to create religious discontent among many people in the United States. The vectors themselves are not new or unique to our own religious experience (they are part of what experts call "religious enculturation"), but the way in which they are being expressed is creating an unusual amount of discontent at this time in this place.

1. A Confusion of Means and End

A religious form or idea gone bad or abused is not a good reason to discard religion altogether. But that's the trick: knowing what to throw away and what to keep. It's the difficulty that has always confronted people interested in the spiritual during times of religious change. It's a matter of identifying means and end. Religion has the potential to speak to deep and fundamental human concerns—that's the end. The means, or way of speaking to those human concerns, changes frequently in form and appearance. When the particular means becomes elevated to the end or goal of religion, trouble can brew. This tug-of-war between means and end is common to all religions, but let me see if I can make it concrete by illustrating from the form of religion I know best—Protestant Christianity.

The Protestant church has always had an element of the entrepreneurial spirit about it. Saddleback, Willow Creek, Calvary Chapel, and the numerous storefront or big-box church structures that dot the North American landscape are all testament to the drive within Protestantism to innovatively meet the felt needs of people within their service area. Thriving and successful church organizations do well in meeting the felt needs of their congregations, using means or expressions that are relevant and timely. On the other hand, church groups that fail to meet those felt needs, remaining locked into expressions that are no longer relevant or capable of communicating, will diminish and shrivel, becoming museum pieces of their former selves. Every city or town in America has church buildings that fit this description. Think of just a few examples of change that have occurred in the past twenty years. The Sunday school picnic, which many of us remember fondly from our childhoods, has been replaced by the food court or coffee and donut station in the church's "Welcome Center." The prayer chain has become email and discussion boards or social networking sites like YouTube and Facebook. The old-fashioned hymn sing is now a concert with stage production, lights, and special effects. All of these events or programs have a place in meeting the real and relevant needs of people. But, when a particular activity loses its ability to meet a need, it changes into something else or it becomes a lifeless remnant of a former time. Say what you will about this Protestant religious entrepreneurism (and there is much to criticize), it does force us to constantly assess the ability of any religious form, idea, or belief to touch people where they are. It forces upon us the question: So what? And this question, if nothing else, clearly exposes the end or purpose of the religious form.

The ability to answer the so-what question with meaningful and deep assistance, providing help to confront some of the most fundamental of all human experiences and aspirations, is what gives religion its draw. Religious talk and rituals touch our deepest parts, connecting us to an eternity broader than ourselves. But religion's great power can quickly and seductively become tyrannical. When a particular way of doing things, which in itself is a culturally conditioned expression of religion (the kind of songs sung, the time or place of church services, the color of carpet on the floor, or even the way in which beliefs are expressed), rises to the level of absolute and timeless imperative it can easily be abused and misused. When so used, religious forms become captive to the lust for power by those persons and institutions controlling that religious expression. An objection to a lust for power is not far below the surface of all the complaints we surveyed at the beginning of this chapter, and that same objection is woven into much of the current spirit of religious discontent sweeping across North America.

2. Belief and Practice Frequently Don't Mix

The charge of hypocrisy has often been leveled at religion and religious people. There's nothing particularly newsworthy about that. But religion doesn't have the corner on this particular vice, and the tension created by conflicting belief and practice can be symptomatic of something more than a religious leader or zealot saying one thing but doing another. The second vector we must examine does involve a tension between belief and practice, but this tension runs deeper than simple hypocrisy.

Most forms of religion embody a tension between the past and the future. On the one hand, religions tend to be conservative, leaning back to an idealized past and attempting to recapture a bygone era when belief was pure and life's dilemmas were simple and clear-cut. The doctrinal statements or statements of belief within a great many Protestant churches, especially the independent and Evangelical Protestant churches in North America, point in that direction. Generally, when it comes to the doctrine of a group, change is viewed suspiciously and the doctrinal statement functions to hold the group anchored to the firm tradition and belief of the past, to the "timeless truths that do not change."

But this view of doctrine or beliefs, as timeless and unchanging, is a conclusion that can only be sustained through the fog of historical distance. The fact of the matter is that most doctrinal statements are born out of conflict, change, and controversy. Rarely do beliefs that appear self-evident to a group make it into that group's statement of faith. There is no need. It's only the controversial issues that need to be made normative and formalized in a statement of faith. For example, the early Christian community seemed to regularly practice speaking in tongues and other similar paranormal behaviors. Everybody did it, so nobody needed convincing by reading about it in a confession or catechism. Now, however, the behavior is not universally practiced and is often challenged, so makes its way into the doctrinal statements of both groups supporting the practice and groups not supporting the practice. Often by default, religious groups use controversial issues like this one to stake out their identity.[3] Or, consider that early in the history of Christianity there was more than a little debate

---

3   Similar examples could be cited involving abortion, capital punishment, the inerrancy of the Bible, the second coming of Jesus, the nature and function of church offices, etc. The ARIS 2008 report affirms the same: "... many millions do not fully subscribe to the theology of the groups with which they identify" (8).

over the humanity of Jesus. Some advocated that he was a phantom of sorts, only appearing to be human. Others insisted that he was just as human as you or me, simply absent the many foibles we embody. The issue was hotly debated, settled, and fell out of view until the late 1700s, when the deity of Jesus once again became an issue by which believers defined themselves. When it was thought everybody believed it, there was no need to include this doctrine in statements of faith. That all changed in the early 1900s with the publication of the *Fundamentals* and a new debate between Protestant Fundamentalism and Protestant Liberalism that would dominate the early part of the twentieth century. The point is, statements of faith are usually responses to a challenge—a challenge that calls into question the legitimacy of this or that belief. It is only with the passage of time that these lists of core beliefs assume an air of inevitability. Statements of belief serve to tie the group to a past in the face of an uncertain and controversial present.

But a religious group is more than a doctrinal statement, and this confessional tie to the past is stretched—sometimes to the breaking point—as the group also attempts to meet needs of real people in a changing and variable present. The conservative nature of faith frequently runs head to head against the innovative nature of practice, and the past finds itself in conflict with the present or the future. In other words, the stated belief of the group doesn't always match the actual practice of the group. In fact, it's rare to run across a church group in which the majority even knows what the group's statement of faith says! When this conflict between faith and practice happens often enough, the stool of religious knowledge develops a wobble and doubt ensues.

Once again the Pew Survey offers helpful information in understanding the present expression of this tension between a religious past and a religious present. The Pew Survey has revealed that there is a broad spectrum of belief even among dedicated churchgoers in the United States. Regarding those items that could be expected to function as core beliefs—how to understand the Bible, the existence of heaven and hell, the character of God—there is remarkable diversity within the same religious group.[4] Given the variety of belief they encountered, the Pew surveyors drilled down a bit further, attempting to discover what was really important in forming attitudes, beliefs, and behaviors among religious adherents of particular religious organizations. Near the top of the list was the frequency of interaction with the larger group. This suggests that it isn't the "doctrine" or "statement of faith" from a church or religious group that influences people but the group itself—the social networks and interpersonal

4   "U.S. Religious Landscape Survey. Religious Beliefs and Practices: Diverse and Politically Relevant," by the Pew Forum on Religion and Public Life (Washington: Pew Research Center, June 2008), 8–14.

interactions that give vitality to the religious form.[5] The group may give lip service to a particular set of beliefs, but when push comes to shove those beliefs have little to do in determining the actual practice of the group. That is, built into the very existence of many religious groups in America is a disparity between faith and practice. If the discrepancy between faith and practice is large enough, the schizophrenic condition becomes more than sufficient to convince many that religion sucks.

3. The Emergence of the Evangelical Subculture has Changed the Religious Formula in America

The third vector helping to create an element of disconcerting religious change in the United States is the constantly shifting alliance between religion and politics. In recent years[6] the reemergence of evangelicalism as a dominant cultural influence has had unintended consequences. Like many religious forms, evangelicalism defines itself, to no small measure, by what it is not. Until very recently Evangelicals have made a name for themselves by being against gay marriage, abortion, big government, gun control, and so forth. As evangelicalism has integrated

---

5   "U.S. Religious Landscape Survey. Religious Beliefs and Practices: Diverse and Politically Relevant," 21.

6   Many look back to the presidential campaign of Jimmy Carter in the mid-1970s as the event ushering evangelicalism back onto the main stage of America's culture.

into the fabric of American culture, its tendency to define itself by what it is not has spilled over into the national self-perception. Evangelicalism gave to American politics a sense of moral rightness, and American politics gave to evangelicalism a sense of respectability and triumphalism. The marriage of American politics and evangelicalism expressed itself in three major themes easily crossing the political/religious divide:[7]

A Dualistic View of Humanity with People and Nations Residing in One of Two Camps: Good or Evil. One of the chief social functions of religion is to discriminate, dividing people into insiders and outsiders. Having defined the outsiders as the evildoers, those not like us, it is very tempting to engage the power of the state in a moral battle to overcome evil.

The Divine Election of the Evangelical United States. God is active in the affairs of humanity through his chosen people. Consequently, whatever enterprise the elect choose to pursue, regardless of its observable moral merits, has the weight of divine approval behind it.

A Deeply Felt Responsibility for the Salvation of the World by Making Outsiders into Insiders. Conversion, with the resultant spread of freedom (a very vague and so very useful term) and law, are worthy activities designed

---

7   Bruce Lincoln, "On Political Theology, Imperial Ambitions, and Messianic Pretensions," in *Belief and Bloodshed: Religion and Violence Across Time and Tradition*, edited James Wellman, 211–225 (New York: Rowman and Littlefield, 2007), 221–222.

to extend the reign of God, even if an apocalyptic end to history is threatened in the process.

Religious sensibilities, given the military power of the state (and increasingly, para-state organizations), can create an imposing force quite capable of shock and awe. Intimidating alliances between religion and politics were commonplace at the beginning of the twenty-first century.

But the uncritical alliance between faith and politics has created a rocky path. When being a "good Christian" and being a "good American" became interchangeable, evangelicalism's tendency to define itself by what it is not began to assume political characteristics reshaping the world into those who were either for America or those who were against America. But it goes both ways. The characteristics of the "outsider" defined by popular notions of what makes a "good American" have seeped into the religious consciousness of the "good Christian," becoming clearly evident in the surge of patriotic (and militaristic) symbols and themes within in the walls of evangelical churches. This changing religious consciousness has the potential to fundamentally redefine religion's expression.[8] Although evangelicalism is usually seen as a phenomenon of Protestant Christianity, evangelicalism's tendency to

---

8   The uncritical alliance between Christianity and capitalism in Europe of the eighteenth century figured prominently into the protests raised by Karl Marx in *Das Kapital*, first published in 1867.

redefine religion according to this or that particular social issue is easily found within Roman Catholicism and other religions as well. Some have concluded that the following set of beliefs now create a universe of religious conviction, representing a redefinition of religion that has already swept across evangelical Christianity in the United States:[9]

- Evangelical conversion will address and solve social problems.

- The government should protect America's religious heritage.

- The United States was founded as a Christian nation.

- It is hard to be a political liberal and a Christian.

- Democracy should be promoted around the world.

- The U.S. should advocate for economic, religious, and political liberty.

---

9   James Wellman Jr., "Is War Normal for American Evangelical Religion?," in *Belief and Bloodshed: Religion and Violence Across Time and Tradition*, edited James Wellman, 195–210 (New York: Rowman and Littlefield, 2007) 197.

- By extension of these last two, the war in Iraq must be supported.

If you find yourself in disagreement with any or several of the above core beliefs, you risk becoming an outsider not only to a particular political point of view, but an outsider to a dominant religious sensibility as well. When a political position can convincingly claim the endorsement of God, it becomes a powerful social force that is resisted only at great cost. The rise of the evangelical movement and its infiltration into political life formed an imposing coalition of the willing in the United States at the turn of the twenty-first century. But recently that coalition has begun to fracture, and the rise of the "unaffiliated" forebodes a change on the horizon. The evangelical political and religious orthodoxy prominent in the first decade of the century is quickly becoming replaced. A new trend will assert itself and then yet another.

YOU'RE NOT ALONE

That change is already here. The most recent information available suggests a polarizing divide is forming with about a third of the population in America in the evangelical camp,[10] about 25 to 30 percent rejecting the idea of a

---

10   ARIS 2008, i. Highlights.

personal God,[11] and the rest somewhere between (including adherents to Judaism, Islam, and other nontraditional forms of religion). The movement toward both ends of the spectrum is something new in American religion.

So, let's draw together the three vectors we just surveyed. First, we need to remember religious changes occur from time to time. Especially when old forms and expressions become deficient in meeting the pressing needs of real people, a sense of religious unease is sure to develop. Add to this unease the recognition that statements of belief easily become out of sync with actual religious practice. It's neither malicious nor even intentional, but these feelings of being out of step can create a sense of disconnect that easily morphs into a perception that religion is irrelevant, or at least without credibility. Finally, understand that religion's place in the public arena is up for grabs, with the interplay between politics and religion creating a constantly moving target. Stir all three vectors together, and it's quite understandable that the firm convictions of only a few years ago are losing their appeal. Any one of these three vectors would be more than enough to create a sense of unease, but when all three collide their impact grows exponentially and many conclude that religion sucks (or at least that America is now post-Christian).

---

11   ARIS 2008, 9.

So What's to Be Done?

For many, the religious trends in the United States and the declining role of religious traditions is a cause for alarm and hand wringing. Jon Meacham can announce the end of Christian America,[12] and James Dobson can pessimistically describe America at the crossroads of history,[13] but there is another way of looking at what's going on around us. While we, Americans, are describing ourselves as less religious, we are at the same time affirming that we are very spiritual. That is, we take matters like God, eternal life, personal meaning and significance, care for the planet, and salvation very seriously. It's just that religion no longer seems to work in communicating those matters. Common to the religious forms that are declining is a top-down model in which religious knowledge is based upon the authority of a church leader, institution, or sacred book. This model of knowledge is being replaced by methods that emphasize personal experience (touching you where you live) and coherence (making sense in the world of today). Religion isn't dying; it's morphing.[14]

---

12   Jon Meacham, "The End of Christian America," *Newsweek* (April 13, 2009).

13   James Dobson, "Dr. Dobson's February Newsletter: America at the Crossroads of History," www.citizenlink.org/focusaction/updates/A000009334. cfm (3/26/09).

14   Recently described in the insightful book by Peter Berger and Anton Zijderveld, *In Praise of Doubt: How to Have Convictions Without Becoming a Fanatic* (New York: HarperOne, 2009).

There are two constants among all human cultures: religion and music. Both have been around for a long time and neither appear to be in threat of disappearing any time soon. So if religion is an unavoidable fact of human culture, and if you find yourself less than pleased with the religious forms you have experienced, what's to be done? Many have chosen to simply bag it, to drop out of religious affiliation and attempt to go it alone. I think this is a viable short-term solution, but it won't work over the long haul. Even the unaffiliated will gradually develop habits and customs, patterns of ritual, that give shape to their spiritual aspirations. Religion simply won't go away.

But if you are less than satisfied with the role of religion in your quest to know God, don't lose heart. Every major religious reform has grown out of spiritual discontent, often fueled by dramatic changes in communication technology (the "twitterization" of God). Reform is happening all around us. That reform is now evidenced in the many varieties of religious expression within Christianity, each seeking to get it right. Christianity can be highly formal and liturgical as with the Roman Catholic, Episcopal, and some Lutheran churches. Or it can be characterized by spontaneity and a sense of organized chaos as in the Pentecostal and community churches. You can find church occupying grand, stately, and inspiring buildings in which solemn decorum is the order of the day. Or you can find church in plain big-box structures housing fast-food courts, bookstores, aerobic centers, and stages complete with sound systems, lights, and smoke machines that would make most rock bands envious. I've seen church in a shopping mall, at highway rest stops, county fairs, and even in a bar. There is the emerging church, the house church movement, the traditional church, electronic church, consumer church, vintage church, green church, and a return to the neighborhood church. The denominational differences of half a century ago are nothing compared to the varieties that characterize Christianity's expression today. All these different expressions of Christianity are attempts to get it right. They are all expressions of religious reform seeking to embody the message of Christianity in a way that makes sense to people. The very fact of the variety is more than enough to indicate that no single form alone will work. So, if you have found religion a bad experience, don't lose heart. There's plenty more to choose from.

Your discontent may simply indicate that you are searching for something more. Unfortunately, that hunger for something more can be threatening to compatriots satisfied with the religious status quo. All too often, religion's emissaries resort to guilt and browbeating in order to produce conformity among spiritual seekers. Conformity is required to support the structures and programs of the institution. Truth be told, many churches need their customers in order to meet budget and so are desperate to retain members for reasons quite mundane and businesslike. The pressure to conform may have nothing to do with an authentic spiritual quest. Don't give in and don't despair of your search.

If there is any reality to the Divine, that reality will be encountered amid your own religious quest. Be bold. You are important to God, and he is seeking you. Augustine, a famous Christian theologian, once admitted to God, "my faith calls on You—that faith which You have imparted to me."[15] It may well be that your search for religious fulfillment is nothing other than the process of God finding you. Although, I admit, the process is sometimes very difficult and there is no guarantee what the end result will look like, there is comfort to be found in the search. The Unseen Companion is more invested in your quest than you or I can know. Your season of discontent may itself be evidence that there is Something more to be discovered.

In pursuit of that discovery there is one more stream we must cross. This one is not easy, and we are about to wade into deep waters. I would not lead you here if I didn't think the journey necessary and the outcome useful. But troublesome as it may be, the next chapter is necessary. So steel yourself, here we go.

---

15 *Confessions of St. Augustine*, Book 1, Chapter 1. The Nicene and Post-Nicene Fathers. First Series. Vol.1. (Grand Rapids, MI: Eerdmans, 1974), 45.

2

The Devastation: Where Was God When the Earth Shook?

December 26 has become a memorial for me, changing radically the celebration of December 25. On December 26, 2004, a horrendous wall of water swept the shores of the Indian Ocean, resulting in the deadliest thirty minutes in all human history. No weapon of war has proven so costly. Even the devastating explosions over Hiroshima and Nagasaki did not snuff out as many lives in such a short period of time. And although the Jewish Holocaust of the twentieth century resulted in a greater loss of life, even the Nazi demons were not able to compact so much carnage into such a short time. Unlike those acts of war, which changed the direction of human events, the tsunami of December 26 can only be described as an "act of God." There is no possible way to shift blame for this deadly event to human shoulders. If an all-powerful God is present in the universe, there is no shirking his responsibility for those fateful thirty minutes. So the tension for me is almost unbearable. On December 25 my religious tradition celebrates a divine incarnation—God with us. Now, on December 26, I mourn the loss of a quarter million people. I mourn the overwhelming grief felt by orphaned children, felt by widows, and felt by parents robbed of their children. And I mourn the loss of my own religious naiveté. I can understand God with us on December 25; it's December 26 that gives me a problem. On December 26, I memorialize the Devastation.

My own religious anxiety was given focus when I happened to attend a church service the Sunday after the tsunami. Two parts of that church experience continue to haunt me. First was the worship service filled with people singing and clapping, celebrating the wonder of a baby born in a manger. There were prayers, a sermon, and lots of talk. But never once was there even a mention of the Devastation. Not a prayer, not an offer of sympathy, not a word. The world of that church experience was impenetrably insulated from the world of the Devastation. I later attended the adult Sunday school session following the worship service. There the tsunami was talked about—but I wish it hadn't been. "If any of them were Christians, they went to heaven" and "Well, most of them weren't Christians so they got what they deserved" were the sentiments expressed in attempting to explain the loss of life. Whether intended or not, the attitude expressed in this large evangelical church was unmistakable. "God with us," the identification of God with humanity, means that we need not be. Religion, as expressed on that day among these people, had become a way to divide people—to show which people God likes and which people he does not. For these church people, the God with us on December 25 was selectively applied only to people *like us* on December 26. For me, the result has been deeply moving. I don't blame Santa Claus for taking "Christ out of Christmas." I think he left on his own.

I wish I could say that this particular church is unique, but I can't. I teach college students for a living, and during the fall semester it has become my habit to devote a class period to exploring the human significance of December 26, 2004. I begin the class period by asking the students (sixty to eighty in attendance) to identify what happened on that fateful day. Usually, less than ten can correctly recall the singular event that took place December 26, 2004. If these young people are representative of and reflect the formative influences in their lives, then I have to conclude that the earthquake spawning the tsunami of December 26, 2004, may have wobbled the earth, but for many from my own religious tradition, it didn't even cause a blink. Although the Devastation has been safely marginalized by some in religious circles, I am not alone in feeling the overwhelming grief caused by the event. The Devastation has left many people shaken to their core.

The December 26 Devastation has been particularly troubling for me, not because of the tragic loss of nearly a quarter million lives, but because of the tragedy of one death—repeated a quarter of a million times. In 2003 my wife, who is also my best friend and the dearest part of my life, was diagnosed with cancer. The depth of pain I felt when contemplating her loss, only now repeated over and over—a quarter million times over—makes the Devastation overwhelming.

And now Haiti. On January 12, 2010, the earth shook again. Best estimates are that 230,000 people perished, while untold numbers were wounded, maimed, and viciously robbed of home, family, and friends. In a land already reeling from hurricanes and poverty, this Great Sadness is just too much. If God is active in the affairs of humanity, the Devastation and Great Sadness are acts of God unparalleled in all of human history. How can it be that a half million people can die, their lives cruelly snuffed out, if a loving God reigns supreme? Our inquiry into knowing God can claim little usefulness if it bypasses a consideration of what the Devastation and Great Sadness reveal to us about a God who acts.

The problem represented by the Devastation has been with us, seemingly, from the beginning of time. The problem of evil or of suffering or of injustice has plagued people (religious and nonreligious) for years. Often the problem results in a polarization, with people gravitating to one camp or another. Yet, for us, it will not do to entertain religious people who simply label others, those who do not agree, as bad or immoral or somehow against God. Neither will it work for nonreligious folk to label the religious as dimwitted or selectively ignoring unsolvable problems of faith in order to flee to a place of false security. Both of these alternatives are equally guilty of intellectual dishonesty and in the long run offer no help. Instead, we have to realize and admit that good people—honest and sincere—have come to different conclusions when struggling with this problem. Two fine examples of honest struggle arriving at different conclusions can be found in books by James Crenshaw and Bart Ehrman.[16] Not only do these two represent two different points of view; they represent good models for how to talk civilly about important concerns.

NOT JUST A MATTER OF THE MIND

Somehow, describing the Devastation as only a tsunami—or the Great Sadness as a simple earthquake, the result of moving tectonic plates—seems totally insufficient, if not absolutely immoral. I remember seeing a photo taken in one of the seaside regions of India after the flood. The picture was of a young boy, no more than five or six, looking directly into the camera—looking directly at me—and

---

16   Two examples of different conclusions offered are by Bart Ehrman, *God's Problem: How the Bible Fails to Answer Our Most Important Question – Why We Suffer* (New York: HarperOne, 2008), and James Crenshaw, *Defending God: Biblical Response to the Problem of Evil* (New York: Oxford University Press, 2005).

weeping uncontrollably as he pulled on the arm of his life-less mother lying still on the ground. No matter how hard he pulled, his mother would not get up. She could not wipe away his tears. She could not comfort him. It would be damnable to talk to this boy about moving tectonic plates. No. A discussion of suffering that engages only the intellect will not do. I am convinced that the only appropriate way for us to talk with one another about the real experience of human suffering is to talk with one another with tears in our eyes. The most authentic and most meaningful ex-changes are when the problem of evil is taken out of the abstract, when it's not just a rational obstacle to overcome or an argument to win, but when this problem of suffering takes on flesh and blood, when it becomes seen in the Devastation or in a diagnosis of serious illness for some-one you love. As we tackle this problem— asking where is God when it hurts—let me encourage you to keep the Devastation and Great Sadness in the back of your mind, and never stray too far from your own experience of suf-fering, tragedy, and death.

Some have found the problem of undeserved suffer-ing—made very concrete in the problems of the Devastation and Great Sadness—too great an obstacle, leading them to disbelief in a particular form of religion or disbelief in the existence of God in general. The problem of suffering simply can't be squared with a belief in an all-loving and all-powerful God. It's troublesome, very troublesome. But perhaps the fact that we find it troublesome indicates that the problem of suffering is a reminder that something is not right. We find the Devastation troubling (or must marginalize it) because we weren't made to find it acceptable. The Devastation shouts to us in a voice that cannot be silenced, telling us that something is wrong. All suffering echoes the same message. We weren't made to find this kind of environment comfortable, and we should resist the lure to give in and get used to it. Violence of all sorts should make us uneasy; it should bother us. It is contrary to the way we were made. But if suffering and violence—if the Devastation—is clear evidence that we are misfits in our universe, why and how did this happen?

DESCRIBING THE PROBLEM

The problem of unjust suffering is the result of a collision that occurs when three fundamental ideas meet together. Those three ideas are captured in the following three assertions:

- God is all loving.

- God is all powerful.

- Undeserved suffering exists.

The acceptance of all three of these assertions is the nexus of the problem we now face. A collision is set up, as illustrated in the following diagram.

The problem at the center of the diagram can be resolved by denying the reality of any one of the three colliding arrows. In a whole variety of ways, that denial has been attempted by many, many people. Below are some of the recurring forms the denial takes.

God isn't really all powerful. This op
in several different variations. Perhaps Go
intervene in the universe he has made. Perhap
ited to helping only the one going through the suffe
could it be that forces of evil have become so domin
the universe that God is limited to a re-creation at the e
of time when all those evil influences will be removed? Or,
perhaps some notion of human "free will" limits the power
God really desires to exercise on behalf of the misguided
sufferer.

Others deny that God is all loving. Those opting for this
resolution suggest there can be no misgiving about the
divine responsibility for things that happen and, like Job,
are led to question whether God has a demonic streak to
him. Although I suspect it would be vigorously denied, it
seems to me that this is the option most religious traditions
select. It certainly is the option chosen by those religious
people I listened to in that church service the Sunday after
the Devastation, and it is certainly the position chosen
by Pat Robertson when he claimed the Great Sadness
a result of a Haitian "pact with the devil" ("Pat Robertson
says Haiti paying for 'pact with the devil,'" CNN: January
13, 2010). The argument goes something like this: If indeed
there is only one Creator, then that Creator must assume
responsibility for everything that exists. His creation is an
expression of his character, so if evil and suffering really

...tion is expressed
...d isn't free to
...s he is lim-
...ring. Or,
...ant in
...d

ə who created existence.
view very clearly:

ness,
ə,
these things.

ᴛne third possibility is to deny the reality of suffering. This, too, can happen in a variety of ways. Sometimes the sting of the reality of suffering is soothed by claiming that the suffering is God's way to teach the sufferer some great good that far outweighs the cost involved. Another way to mitigate the reality of the suffering is to claim that the suffering is more than made up for by some future reward. Still others assert that our perspective is wrong. That when we attempt to take in the big picture, the suffering of the individual is in reality part of some grand mosaic that, on a much larger scale, is actually part of a whole and beautiful good being fashioned by God.

Thus, in one way or another, many seek a resolution to the dilemma posed by unjust suffering and the experience of evil by attempting to remove one or more of the colliding arrows illustrated in the diagram above. The biblical writers are no exception, and it is worth our while to pause a moment to survey the various solutions offered by those writers to their readers.

Why Do People Suffer? The Variety of Biblical Answers[17]

Suffering Is a Just Result and Punishment for Sin

At its most basic level, this answer, found often through-out the Bible, suggests that suffering is caused by God as punishment for sin and disobedience. Perhaps one of the clearest and most concise expressions of this position is found in Deuteronomy 28. Quite clearly, obedience brings certain and specific results (verses 1–14), as does disobe-dience (verses 15–68). The principle has been labeled "just recompense" and asserts that people get what they deserve—either good or bad. The principle is maintained throughout the narrative of ancient Israel contained in the books of Joshua, Judges, Samuel, and Kings and is also characteristic of several of the prophetic books (for example, Isaiah and Amos). But even here the principle works only when a sense of proportionality is maintained. Perhaps a flat tire is a just punishment if you fail to stop your car to let an elderly woman cross the street in front of you. But is the death of all the firstborn children really deserved because of the stubbornness of their political leader (Exodus 11:4–10), especially when the stubbornness seems to have been divinely provoked (Exodus 11:10)? Or, should men die in battle because one of their compatriots,

---

17   Ehrman provides a convenient summary of the solutions offered by the biblical authors in *God's Problem*, 274–276.

in a fashion hidden to all the others, kept a fancy and stylish coat all for his own that had been looted from the conquered town of Jericho (Joshua 7:4–21)?

The difficulties raised by this last example from Joshua lead to a further development in the idea that suffering is a just result of sin. The argument goes: Sin separates the sinner from God. And when an individual is separated from God, the goodness, kindness, and other positive and beneficial attributes and characteristics associated with God are removed only to be replaced by their opposite, with tragic consequences. The condition is not limited to one or two rebellious people, but like a virus or cancer, these harmful and destructive consequences spread throughout the universe. The book of Romans provides the clearest biblical example of this principle. In Romans 5:12 (NRSV) we read, "Therefore, just as sin came into the world through one man, and death came through sin, and so death spread to all because all have sinned."

Implicit in this view, that suffering is the result of sin, is the idea that people are free to choose to engage in behaviors that are sinful or behaviors that are not sinful. A view of human free will stands behind the assertion that suffering is a just consequence for bad behavior.

When used indiscriminately, this proposed solution compounds the problem by layering guilt on top of the suffering. Following the model established by this notion of "reaping what you sow," should any of us experience misfortune or suffering, our first instinct must be to assume that we deserve the ill treatment. We are only getting our just reward.[18] This was certainly the belief of those church people I listened to in that Sunday school session following the Devastation. Even though I, too, have participated in this way of thinking, I find it abhorrent. What great ill could that little Indian boy have possibly committed to merit the anguish expressed on his face as he vainly labored to rouse his fallen mother?

The impossibility and perverseness of the question ending the previous paragraph leads to a variation of the principle. This variation insists that not only do we suffer the consequences for our own bad behavior; we suffer at the hands of other people who act badly as well. It is obvious to us all that we suffer because of our own actions, and, in addition, we often suffer because of the maltreatment of others. The point of this line of argumentation, however, is simply to assert it's not God's fault.

The line of reasoning goes: To create a good and perfect world, the all-powerful and all-loving Creator created a universe in which we were given the opportunity to authentically experience love. The authentic experience of love must also include the freedom by which we choose to love or not to love, for love coerced or devoid of choice is

---

18   On at least three occasions Jesus disavows this line of reasoning, arguing instead that there is no necessary connection between natural catastrophe and moral standing (Matthew 5:45; Luke 13:1–4; John 9:1–3).

not love at all. As can be confirmed by just about everyone's experience, more often than not, love has been rejected with all-too-obvious tragic consequences.

This option resolves our dilemma by effectively limiting the power of God by inserting the "free will" of the human agent. God may want to step in and fix things (all loving) but he restrains himself out of respect for the authentic ability to choose, with which he has gifted his creation.

Suffering Has a Good Outcome

At times, the biblical writers present suffering as a path leading to a greater good either for the one suffering or for others who benefit by the suffering of someone else. The "no pain, no gain" mantra repeated by athletes in training finds a parallel among the biblical writers. Sometimes this idea is seen in the hope that suffering will bring about repentance and lead to a greater enjoyment of God's blessings. This idea can be found in the "Song of Moses" of Deuteronomy 32.

> See now that I, even I, am he,
> And there is no god beside me;
> I kill and I make alive;
> I wound and I heal;
> And there is none that can deliver out of my
> hand. (Deuteronomy 32:39)

The hope is for a "healing" that follows the wound. The same idea is offered as a note of hope by many of the prophets. The prophet Amos illustrates quite well:

> In that day I will raise up
> The booth of David that is fallen
> And repair its breaches,
> And raise up its ruins,
> And rebuild it as in the days of old. (Amos 9:11)

The prophet Isaiah inserts the idea that suffering can lead to benefit for others. The Suffering Servant of chapter 53 provides material taken up once again by several New Testament writers (Matthew 8:17; 1 Peter 2:24–25).

> Surely he has borne our griefs
> And carried our sorrows;
> Yet we esteemed him stricken,
> Smitten by God, and afflicted.
> But he was wounded for our transgressions,
> He was bruised for our iniquities;
> Upon him was the chastisement that made us whole,
> And with his stripes we are healed. (Isaiah 53:4–5)

And although this notion of suffering for others is applied preeminently to Jesus, this view of suffering isn't limited to the redemptive work of Jesus. Paul, in 2 Corinthians 1:3–6, interprets some of his own mistreatment as a means of benefiting other people.

Suffering Is to Test Our Faith

A variation on the theme of the benefits of suffering is that suffering can be a very useful educational tool. Some biblical writers suggest that suffering has the potential of a greater good by instructing the sufferer in a more moral and pious lifestyle. Like the suggestion above ("Suffering Has a Good Outcome"), this idea, emphasizing the educational value of suffering, reduces the real condition of suffering by suggesting that it is, in the end, a good thing in disguise. The conversation between God and Satan in the prologue of Job presupposes this value given to suffering.

> And the LORD said to Satan, "Have you considered my servant Job, that there is none like him on earth, a blameless and upright man, who fears God and turns away from evil? He still holds fast to his integrity, although you moved me against him, to destroy him without cause." (Job 2:3)

The New Testament, too, includes instances of this explanation for suffering. Once again, the suffering of Jesus is submitted to this rationale. Hebrews 5:8 says, "Although he was a Son, he learned obedience through what he suffered."

But it isn't just the suffering of Jesus that is explained in this manner. Paul suggested to the Philippians that through his experiences of suffering he learned "I can do all things in him who strengthens me" (Philippians 4:13). Another well-known reference seems to suggest that all believers can "prove what is the will of God, what is good and acceptable and perfect" through a process that involves, in part at least, an element of sacrifice (Romans 12:1–2).

This idea—that the benefits of suffering outweigh the tragedy of the suffering—is not limited to biblical exposition. Most famously, Friedrich Nietzsche[19] coined a proverb now used by many self-help groups: "That which doesn't kill me makes me stronger." While that may be true in some instances (the discipline learned through hard work or the athletic prowess developed through rigorous training, or even the sacrifice spoken of by Paul), it is difficult to see how this idea has any relevant bearing for the majority of people suffering horrendous heartaches so common to us all. This idea of the benefits of suffering may work in

---

19   Friedrich Nietzsche, *Twilight of the Idols and the Anti-Christ: or How to Philosophize with a Hammer*, originally 1888, translated by R. J. Hollingdale (New York: Penguin Classics, 1990).

some cases, but certainly not in all. Should I tell the little boy pulling on the arm of his dead mother that this is really for his own good or that somebody else will be improved because of his anguish? In my opinion, nothing could be more hellish.

Suffering Is a Result of the Forces of Evil Warring Against God

This notion—that the created universe has been invaded by beings, evil and sinister in their design, warring against the good providence of God—is seen in a very limited fashion in the early part of Job 2, which we looked at a little earlier. In the New Testament, the idea is given full expression. Principalities, powers, and authorities—spirit beings in active conflict with God—work their unpleasantness among us and are the cause of evil and suffering. Jesus and Paul, in particular, conceived of suffering as a consequence of the unrestrained activity of evil forces that had come to hold sway over the world of humanity. These evil beings and forces, powers and authorities, were, for Jesus and Paul, working their evil designs, harming people and creation, in rebellion to the Creator God. Their "revolt against heaven" is temporary, however, and in the end, order and righteousness will be restored as God regains control over the cosmos and rescues his chosen ones from the present power of sin and death.

> For we are not contending against flesh
> and blood, but against principalities, against
> the powers, against the world rulers of this
> present darkness, against the spiritual
> hosts of wickedness in the heavenly places.
> (Ephesians 6:12)

It isn't just the human realm that has been affected by the negative influence of this revolt against heaven. The very fabric of the cosmos has been harmed, necessitating nothing less than a total remake of the universe in order to bring the warfare to an end. This is exactly the prescription described in those apocalyptic sections of the Bible, both Old Testament and New.[20] Daniel is clear in his view that the reassertion of divine rule will be inaugurated through the efforts of God's chosen Messiah (Daniel 7:14), a theme used broadly in the New Testament to explain the life, death, and resurrection of Jesus.

> Jesus said to them, "Truly, I say to you, in the
> new world, when the Son of man shall sit on
> his glorious throne, you who have followed
> me will also sit on twelve thrones, judging
> the twelve tribes of Israel. And every one

---

20   This idea is not limited to the biblical writers. The Samaritans maintain hope in the appearance of the Taheb, a messianic figure from God who will restore the era of Divine Favor, lost during a time of Israel's apostasy.

who has left houses or brothers or sisters or
father or mother or children or lands, for my
sake, will receive a hundredfold, and inherit
eternal life. (Matthew 19:28–29)

At least within the biblical material, this apocalyptic
vision is taken to its fullest in the book of Revelation. There,
a lake of fire is described that will ultimately consume
Satan and his cohorts, all the wicked, and even Death
itself (Revelation 20). Finally, the dilemma of unjust suffering is forever resolved by the creation of a new heaven
and a new earth in which "he [God] will wipe away every
tear from their eyes, and death shall be no more, neither
shall there be mourning nor crying nor pain any more, for
the former things have passed away" (Revelation 21:4).

Meanwhile, this warfare isn't hopeless, for an end is in
sight in which the rightful, loving, and powerful presence
of God will be reasserted.

For I am sure that neither death, nor life, nor
angels, nor principalities, nor things present,
nor things to come, nor powers, nor height,
nor depth, nor anything else in all creation,
will be able to separate us from the love
of God in Christ Jesus our Lord. (Romans
8:38–39)

The Dilemma of Suffering Is Unsolvable

As thrilling as the hope of a new cosmos, devoid of pain and suffering, truly is, this vision offers compensation in the future but does not resolve the dilemma now. In fact, the strength of the apocalyptic vision for the future rests in the acknowledgment of the present suffering. If there were no tears to wipe away, the hope that those tears will one day vanish would hold no appeal. In the apocalyptic vision, the dilemma of the three colliding assertions can only be resolved by creating a new reality in which one of the assertions (the reality of suffering) is removed. In a way, then, the apocalyptic vision leads us to the last position taken by the biblical writers concerning unjust suffering, that is, that there is no resolution. It's either at best an unsolvable mystery, or at worst an indicator that life is absurd.

The writer of Ecclesiastes is intent on finding out if life holds any meaning. In no small measure, because of the very real and tangible fact of suffering (the book uses the word *oppression*) the writer of Ecclesiastes concludes life is "vanity of vanities"[21] (absurd).

> Again I saw all the oppressions that are
> practiced under the sun. And behold, the

---

21   In biblical Hebrew, the formula x of x is the way to express the superlative. Here "vanity of vanities" expresses the utmost vanity.

> tears of the oppressed, and they had no
> one to comfort them! On the side of their
> oppressors there was power, and there was
> no one to comfort them. And I thought the
> dead who are already dead more fortunate
> than the living who are still alive; but bet-
> ter than both is he who has not yet been.
> (Ecclesiastes 4:1–3)

In other words, better off dead, and better still to have never been born. This problem of suffering is very real for the writer of Ecclesiastes, and that assessment is affirmed by a second writer, adding a postscript to the end of the book (12:9–14). For the writer of this postscript, there is no rational resolution to the problem caused by indiscriminate suffering, and so there is nothing else but to "fear God and keep his commandments" (12:13).

Job may be the best-known example of suffering considered an unsolvable mystery. In the course of the conversations between Job and his friends, found throughout the middle part of the book, some of the other alternatives to suffering's dilemma are considered and rejected. Job has not sinned and so his suffering received as just punishment simply will not do. The intensity of the suffering negates any educational or spiritual growth value that the suffering may hold for Job. Further, he will not consider that God has been preempted by an evil power and so take God off the hook for causing his current misery (a position the reader, too, must affirm, for even in the prologue, Satan can only act at the behest and permission of God). Job is left with the full impact of the dilemma we have been considering:

> It is all one; therefore I say,
> He destroys both the blameless and the wicked.
> When disaster brings sudden death,
> He mocks at the calamity of the innocent.
> (Job 9:22–23)

Job's despair takes him through the full gamut of emotions, at times expressing itself in bitter self-loathing (9:21); contemplations of suicide (chapter 10); and vehement, scorching accusations directed at God (chapter 12). In response to Job's challenge, God answers Job from out of the tempest in a most unexpected way (chapters 38–41). God addresses himself directly to Job,[22] paying no attention to the friends—God's would-be defenders and exponents of some of the various views for suffering's cause. Confronted by the magnificence of the vision, Job can only stammer a few words of apology and repentance (40:3–5; 41:1–3, 5). But it's enough. The only reproach Job feels is that of having spoken lightly concerning things

---

22   Within the scope of the biblical literature, this kind of Divine-human encounter is a most unusual and often very dangerous encounter.

he did not understand. God's speech and demonstration conveys, at the most, only mild rebuke. God gives Job no condemnation, but instead takes him on a galactic tour in which Job is shown just how incomplete and partial has been his understanding of the Divine. In other words, the dilemma felt acutely by Job—and by us when considering the Devastation—is not met with new information, making the problem vanish away; but rather, the problem is met only by trust. Job's appeal for more information is met with a divine response: "Trust me."[23]

SUFFERING AND THE QUESTION OF GOD

The biblical writers struggled mightily with the fact of undeserved suffering. It wasn't until the Enlightenment and its aftermath, however, that the difficulties posed by undeserved suffering led many to question the existence of God. At times, the biblical presentation is very pragmatic. Nobody wants to get on God's bad side, and so it seemed only prudent to use whatever clues available, even those derived from the experience of suffering, to learn how to stay off God's black list. At other times, however, the biblical authors are a bit loftier in their designs. Their experience of suffering drove them to God, sometimes in desperation, sometimes in wonder. But through it all, there

---

23   Also Psalm 73.

is no evidence that the experience of suffering led them to question whether God in fact was there at all.[24]

Now it's different. The collision of the three assertions, with which we began this chapter, leads to an intellectual riddle whose only possible resolution is in the death of God. That is, since undeserved suffering cannot be denied, the only resolution is in the refutation of either the all-powerful or all-loving God. This is what happened in the middle part of the twentieth century. This "God"—characterized chiefly as all powerful and all loving, a product of logical consistency derived from the implicit fundamental belief that our universe is a reasonable and closed system of cause and effect—could no longer be sustained under careful scrutiny, and so this God was pronounced dead. The thing is, this ideal and logically persuasive God isn't the God written about by the biblical writers. They never engage only their reason when wrestling with the problem of undeserved suffering. For the biblical writers, as for many of us, the discussion of suffering seems perverse, twisted, and wholly repugnant when engaging only our minds while leaving our emotions and sense of morality behind.

The point is, if we are to take the biblical proposals seriously, knowing that the biblical authors offered their respective solutions, often with full awareness of the other alternatives, we must conclude that the problem of unjust

---

24   Although the writer of Ecclesiastes seems, at times, to vacillate in his confidence.

suffering is not a problem like a mathematical equation, requiring only the mustering of the right variables and arranging them in the proper order to arrive at the desired solution. No, the problem of unjust suffering doesn't work that way. One answer isn't applicable at all times in all places and in all circumstances. There is no "one size fits all" when it comes to the problem of pain.

This conclusion, too, is present in the pages of the biblical offerings. As we have seen, the writers of Ecclesiastes and the middle part of Job, in particular, find all of the conventional answers to the problem of suffering limited and partial in their application. Yet, their response is not to simply conclude: "Aha, I told you; there is no God!" No, for some reason, their inability to figure it all out leads them back to God. To be sure, they don't hesitate to throw their hands up in exasperation or offer an occasional curse borne out of frustration. But in the end, this problem is simply deposited at the feet of the mysterious and intrusive God—the God who takes pleasure in the work of his hands. There is no avoidance in their actions, no pretend or wishing it away, and no blind acceptance. Instead, these writers, who submit the problem of suffering to the mysterious presence of God, agree to live in a tension formed by trust.

These writers of biblical books have come to accept that "God" is not shorthand for a means of resolving life's problems. They seem to accept that God, too, is a free agent not bound by mathematical formulae. They also accept that unresolved dilemmas are no more an argument against the existence of God than are the tensions and contradictions in the personalities of our close friends arguments for their nonexistence. In fact, it may be that one of the important distinctions between our pretend childhood companions and the real ones we now enjoy is that the pretend friends held no surprises and no contradictions. They always acted just as we expected, were always predictable, and never disappointed. Real people are quite different. Real people, no matter how well they are known, always hold surprises. I suspect the same is true with our pretend gods and the real God. Certainly, the acceptance of all three colliding assertions, from our earlier diagram, poses an irresolvable logical problem. But that irresolvable logical problem (like a mathematical formula that simply will not add up) is quite a different matter from concluding there is no God. I would be quite mistaken to conclude that my wife and very best friend doesn't exist simply because she acts contrary to my idea of how a wife and friend should act. It may be a wiser course to accept that my ideal—though the best I can do at the moment—is faulty.

CREATOR, LOVER, REDEEMER

If the irresolvable problem of unjust suffering leads to trust, what are the characteristics of a God we are led to trust? The repeating and loudest descriptions of God offered in the Bible are Creator, Lover, Redeemer. We will examine at length this tri-faceted description in Part 3 of this book. For now, let me suggest that it's the complex of all three (Creator, Lover, Redeemer) wrapped up in one person that meets us in our desperateness. When applying these dominating characteristics of God to the problem of underserved suffering, we are led first to an affirmation that the problem is not solvable and second to a kind of worshipful wonder that inspired the writers of Ecclesiastes, Job, and several of the psalms.

God is Creator. In our diagram, this one divine characteristic affirms two of the three converging lines. The Creator is, in the final accounting, responsible for what is made and so seems to function as all powerful. But the notion of Creator, if taken seriously, must affirm the reality of what is created; and so the reality of suffering cannot be argued away or "phantomized" in any meaningful fashion. Even subjecting the present suffering to a future compensation, when everything is set right, won't do. Suffering isn't like a bitter teaspoon of medicine whose taste can be nullified by an equal or greater amount of sugar or some other sort of compensation. The effort to compensate simply begs the question, Why suffering in the first place? Therefore, to this point the biblical description of God as Creator affirms, rather than refutes, the diagram by which we earlier set up an understanding of our problem caused by undeserved suffering.

God is Lover. This characteristic of God is detailed in the Bible no less than the characteristic we just encountered. In fact, on more than one occasion, God is simply stated to be love.[25] If we think back to our opening diagram, certainly, the characterization of God as Lover affirms the third leg of our colliding matrix—that God acts in a loving manner. So, at this point we are back where we started. The problem is real and the diagram set up earlier in this chapter seems to have no way out.

God is Redeemer. The third characterization of God, Redeemer, may add a twist in our understanding of the dilemma caused by undeserved suffering that may lead us to seriously consider the viewpoint of Ecclesiastes and the middle part of Job. The divine Redeemer not only erases the offense of the forgiven but repairs and welcomes back, renews and cherishes the relationship with the forgiven. The Redeemer restores and repairs, making new and whole, for he re-creates and loves the redeemed. In many ways, the biblical portrait of creation and redemption are simply the opposite sides of the same coin. Creation implies redemption, and redemption is fundamentally a creative act. When applied to the problem of suffering,

---

25   First John 4:7–8 is probably the most explicit statement, although a quasi-creedal statement of the same or very near intent is repeated throughout the Old Testament. See, for example, Exodus 34:6–7 and Deuteronomy 7:9.

the insertion of this third dynamic characteristic of God (never operating in isolation from the other two) presents the possibility, at least, of encountering the unsolvable problem of unjust suffering with hope. The hope is not in a future compensation for present suffering. Nor is the hope for granting some critical piece of information that will enable us to make sense of undeserved suffering. No, the hope offered by this third characteristic of God is that our unsolvable dilemma will also someday be redeemed. Redemption is not simply the notion that I will go to heaven when I die. No, the biblical portrait of redemption proudly exclaims that every part of me will be made right—remade and re-created. All of my hopes, dreams, fears, disappointments, sufferings, and unsolvable dilemmas are redeemed by the Creator, Lover, and Redeemer. And it's important to remember this redemption comes from outside—it's an invasion into the cosmos, not simply a self-correcting righting of a universe gone wrong.

Here's the crux. The object of hope identified and cherished by many of the biblical writers is not a thing, an event, or a time off in the future. That is, the hope offered is not in a particular resolution to our problem of suffering. Instead, hope is first and foremost in God himself—not in a projected and anticipated activity of God. The Creator, Lover, and Redeemer is the source and object of hope. The anguish of undeserved suffering, the Devastation, and the diagnosis of serious illness for someone dearly loved is not met by a celestial course in logic or in pious ritual. The dilemma resulting from the collision of the three arrows we saw earlier, in the diagram by which we began this chapter, is met only with a divine "Trust me."

For many, though, this is not enough.

A God Who Is Near

Some of those for whom the divine response is insufficient are given voice in the Bible itself. Their reluctance is articulated in prayer. The prayers in the Bible, particularly those given expression in the Psalms, are very frequently expressions of desperate individuals confronted by unsolvable dilemmas and tragedy. Their prayers give voice to the unsolvable and petition God for relief. Sometimes the relief is expressed in the form of hope. This hope, voiced in prayer, is often a petition for God to be "near." It's not that the psalmist envisions God, in some mystical fashion, relocating himself in order to sidle up next to the one in difficulty. No, the hope for God to be near is a request for God to make plain and clear his characteristics of Creator, Lover, and Redeemer. It's a prayer and a hope that God will empathize with the one praying. It's a prayer for God to bring relief, in a tangible form, consistent with his character as Creator, Lover, and Redeemer. But please remember it's a prayer. Sometimes the God who is near is difficult to find.

I'll readily admit, this is both my prayer and my terrible anger when I consider the Devastation. I celebrated the God who is near—"God with us"—on December 25, but searched for him in vain on December 26. Where was God when the tides surged? At this point, the best I can do is listen to what has been for me God's repeated response: "Trust me." So on December 25, I celebrate the God with us, and on December 26 I pray:

> Save me, O God!
> For the waters have come up to my neck. . . .
> I have come into deep waters,
> And the flood sweeps over me. . . .
> My eyes grow dim with waiting for my God.
> (Psalm 69:1–3)
> For that little boy, struggling to rouse his
> fallen mother, save him, O God!
> From the blindness caused by our own reli-
> gious arrogance, save us, O God!
> Save me, O God!

Our search for a hole in the sky begins with nothing more than a cry into the void.

Part 2
Can you Get There
From Here?

Our search for a hole in the sky must begin somewhere. For many, that search begins in the discontent
and all-too-real difficulties we examined in Part 1. For all
of us, our search for a hole in the sky begins not in some
abstract or rarified world of ideas, but amid real life. And
sometimes life can be overwhelming. The constant press
of the everyday and routine—interrupted by moments of
joy as well as by episodes of pain and tragedy that seem
to have no end—threatens to push aside any hope of a
meaningful connection with the Deity. The thing is, and
this is where it gets messy, the two are really related.
The daily stuff of life will help shape our understanding of
God, and our relationship with God will certainly affect our

perception of the world around us. And so we must stop. Put everything on hold for just a few minutes. Be willing to ask hard questions of things we thought we knew and see if indeed we can find that hole in the sky in a way that makes sense for us here and now.

3

Real Men Don't Need Directions and Real Women Never Get Lost

> These are mere words—until you believe them. Once believed, they become part of the very apparatus of your mind, determining your desires, fears, expectations, and subsequent behavior.... There seems, however, to be a problem with some of our most cherished beliefs about the world: they are leading us, inexorably, to kill one another.[26]

With this observation, Sam Harris began his discussion of the important and increasingly terrifying role that religious belief plays in the complex of human social interactions. Its frequent violent expression means we can no longer allow religious belief to plead immunity from scrutiny simply because it is religious. The dark side of religious belief—expressing itself in suicide bombings, hate killings, mutilations, child rape, sectarian warfare, beheading, and

---

26   Sam Harris, *The End of Faith: Religion, Terror, and the Future of Reason* (New York: W.W. Norton, 2005), 12.

stonings—is all too evident to anyone with the nerve to watch the nightly news or read a daily paper. And flying under the radar of the national media is the growing intolerance and bigotry expressed within the respectable religious establishments across the United States. Progressively, religion is used as a means of social separation, identifying those whom God likes and those he doesn't like, often with tragic consequences.[27] Although Harris has received more than a fair amount of criticism for what he has written (and an equal amount of acclaim), he isn't making this up. So, if our goal is to know God, and if that knowledge touches the realm of religious belief, we need to examine *how* we know before we proceed to *what* we know.

CHOOSING A PLACE TO START

Others have been down this road before, and we do well to consider the signs they have left for us to follow. John Calvin, a significant religious thinker and formative influence on the Protestant Reformation, wrote an important theology book in the middle part of the sixteenth century titled *Institutes of the Christian Religion*.[28] Calvin

---

27   A social function of religion that Harris addresses, at least in part, in his *Letter to a Christian Nation* (New York: Vintage Books, 2008), ix. Religious polarization appears to be a growing phenomenon in the twenty-first century.
28   Reprinted as John Calvin, *Institutes of the Christian Religion*, translated by Ford Lewis Battles, 2 vols. (Philadelphia: Westminster, 1960), vol. 1, 36–39.

was a trained lawyer and extremely systematic. Detailed logical presentation is evident all through his book. Right off, Calvin began his theology by considering an important problem. He vacillated back and forth, attempting to find the proper place to begin his logical and tightly packed theology. Should he begin talking about God and so risk being blinded and partial simply by the very fact of human limitations? Or, should he begin by describing the human condition and so run the risk of leaving out the most important parts of human existence by limiting himself to only what can be seen with the eye or touched with the hand? In the end, Calvin opted to begin by describing humanity in relation to God and from that springboard simply dove in. While we are not going to struggle with the matter to the degree he did, Calvin was right: beginning points are important. Often, where you begin influences, if not determines, where you end up. If where we want to end up is with a way to know and think about God, where we begin matters. So let's think about where we are now.

It's been said that the best theology is in part autobiography. I think it's true. Frankly, it seems to me pointless at best and a cruel game at worst to consider a God who is beyond our encounter and knowable only in the abstract. A God who cannot be felt or talked with or relied upon seems to me of little use. If what we talk about in reference to God cannot be confirmed, to a degree at least, by encounter—by autobiography—then what's the point? A "God" who is only shorthand for religious mind games and logical gymnastics but who can never be spoken to or met at our most crucial moments doesn't seem to be worth the effort. At heart, this is what Calvin was saying by the way he began his theology: humanity in relation to the Divine. That's where we will begin as well.

READING THE SIGNS IN THE SKY

As we proceed down the path of encounter with God, we will take stock of the tools we have at our disposal, the equipment available to aid us on the way. We need to think together about how we know God, how we determine true and right things about God. In the next few pages we will consider three "signs in the sky" or road signs that can be helpful to us in our quest to know God. The three signs we will think about are not the only ones people have used in knowing God. I chose to focus on these three because I have found these most helpful, and I think you may find them helpful too.

A WORD ABOUT THE BIBLE

Before we look at the three signs helping us in knowing God, let me say a word or two about the Bible. As I indicated in the introduction, I have found the Bible a very helpful book. But before you write me off as simply another Bible-thumping dogmatist seeking to convince everyone how right I am, give me thirty seconds to explain. For right now, let's lay aside the whole issue of the Bible as the Word of God or some authoritative document to be interpreted according to a certain set of religious beliefs. At this point, all I'm suggesting is that the Bible includes documents written by some very smart people who have some important things to say about the human experience. For years and years a whole lot of people have concluded that what the Bible writers have to say is worth listening to. I'm not telling you to accept what I'm saying simply because I characterize it as "based on the Bible." All I'm suggesting is that within the pages of the Bible a whole host of voices are speaking to the reader. Those voices represent a variety of life experiences, viewpoints, and opinions regarding some of the most important fundamental aspects of human experience. And this business of how to know God is chief among the topics the Bible writers opine over. When you boil down all of their direction, advice, and descriptions about God, three different ways to know God stand out: authority, coherence, and experience.

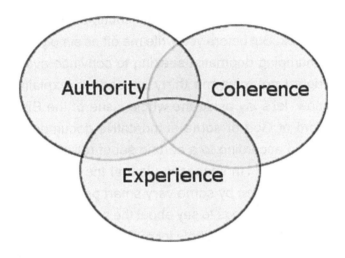

This diagram, with three interlocking spheres, attempts to represent the way in which these three paths to knowledge of God work for the biblical writers. At times, one or another of the spheres dominates, but generally the three are interdependent. Let's take a close look at the three spheres of knowing God used by the Bible writers.

Sign #1: Authority

The first sphere representing a path by which to know God is authority. One of the most easily seen examples of this sphere in action is in the Exodus 20 rendition of the Ten Commandments. In Exodus 20, the commandments are to be received as true simply because God said so. We are to accept the Ten Commandments because they came to us based upon the authority of having been spoken by God. Exodus 20:1 prefaces the ten moral commands by stating quite clearly "God spoke." In Exodus 20, the Ten Commandments are presented as an accurate representation of how God wants people to behave. I can take the commandments as accurate moral directives based upon the authority of the person who communicated them—God.

I realize we could get all caught up in asking, "Did God really say those things, or did somebody just write the Ten Commandments in a book somewhere and try to pawn it off as God's voice?" It's an important question, and one we'll save for a little later (chapter 5). For us right now, it's enough to simply recognize that the Ten Commandments are presented on the basis of divine authority as the foundation for knowing something about God. What is really surprising, especially for those who are relatively new to the Bible, is that this authoritative "God card" is played very infrequently. This direct voice of God serving as an authority by which we can know something about God appears very seldom in the pages of the Bible. Much more common is knowledge about God based upon the authority of a prophet, priest, or some other experienced and recognized expert. The divine authority is mediated by a human agent who becomes authoritative based upon his or her mediation of the divine authority. The priest and sacred scroll are authoritative, not in and of themselves, but because they represent the Divine. Even the proverbial "parent" can suffice as a reliable source upon which to form knowledge of God—sometimes, at least. But none of these mediated or derived authorities are ever granted status simply because of their self-proclaimed position of authority. Tests—particularly tests of character—were applied to evaluate the reliable nature of the authority figure. The quality of life and moral integrity these guides demonstrated were used to verify their claim to authority in knowledge about God. Authority that earns (rather than demands) respect is the kind of authority that is sometimes relied upon by the writers of the Bible in their quest to know God.

So, while there is room for knowing God based upon the authority of some recognized expert or guide, it seems wise to remember and apply the test of authority that we find used in the pages of the Bible. When considering knowledge of God, the information we gain through an authority must be sifted through the question: Is it reliable? As we search for God, we will need to repeatedly evaluate the reliability of the authority figure by examining the moral integrity and character of the guide.

This matter of religious authority is of particular interest to those of us looking for a hole in the sky at the beginning of the twenty-first century. The formula used to produce religious knowledge involves a mix of our three ingredients: authority, coherence, and experience. That mix is changing as reliance on authorities (a religious system, dogmatic theology, or official spokesperson) decreases. This change is deep and promises to be long lasting (the afore mentioned "twitterization" of God). For religious organizations built around a central or top-down authority structure, this change is threatening and does not bode well for the continuance of the organization. Those within the authority structure accuse others of "picking and choosing" or experiencing religion "cafeteria style." They complain that others are only adhering to religious practices or believing religious tenets that are convenient and comfortable.

Let me suggest these complaints have got it wrong. The change in religious understanding has little to do with comfort or convenience. It is much more fundamental than that and far more than a simple acceptance of this or that religious dogma or idea. Authority figures of all sorts are losing their influence, and religious organizations relying upon their own historic authority are now in a long-term and sharp decline. For, it's the concept of authority itself that is being challenged in a progressively "pluralized" world in which religious affiliation is a matter of choice.[29] But this doesn't mean others aren't taking religious matters seriously. Just the opposite! Rather than deferring to some external authority, those searching to know God are much more proactive, seeking a knowledge that is

---

29   Peter Berger and Anton Zijderveld, *In Praise of Doubt: How to have Convictions Without Becoming Fanatic* (New York: HarperOne, 2009), 17–24. See also, Jeffrey Stout, *Democracy and Tradition* (Princeton, NJ: Princeton University Press, 2004).

relevant, understandable, and practical. It's because they are so serious about their search that they are willing to pick and choose, operate cafeteria style, in order to find an authentic link with God.

Sign #2: Coherence

In some ways, the failure of authority figures to pass the test of reliability lends credence to a second path to knowing God found in the Bible: coherence. Think of the coherence path as a check and balance to the first. If the question asked of authorities is, Are they reliable? the question asked by the would-be knower of God using the path of coherence in forming knowledge is, Does it make sense? That is, knowledge of God (or, for that matter, knowledge about any part of the human experience) is tested against the backdrop of an already accepted body of knowledge forming a coherent view of reality.

There are many examples of the coherence path to knowledge of God found in the Bible. In Exodus 3–4 the dispirited and exiled Moses is about to have his world radically reshaped. He encounters God in quite an unusual manner: a burning and talking bush. Through the encounter, his initial skepticism is overcome and he gains new insights into the nature and character of God. Little by little, his conversation with God tests the new information by fitting it into Moses' preexisting coherent view of how the universe was thought to work. The end of the encounter brings Moses to a very different place, a very different understanding of God; but this change was gradual, altering his coherent view of the universe rather than tearing that coherent view apart.

This coherence test was often used by the people who compiled the book of Proverbs. In Proverbs 6:6, the lazy person is encouraged to go and observe the world of the ant. The insect's industrious labors, readily observable to anyone who simply takes the time to watch, provides the context from which to draw moral lessons. The observable insect world, itself fitting into a coherent understanding of the universe around us, provides the entry point for the addition of a new bit of moral advice. What is already known provides the springboard for accepting new knowledge. The same is found in the extended advice concerning the perils of prostitution in chapter 5 of Proverbs and is seen easily in the repeated warnings against laziness in 24:30–34. This process of forming new knowledge based upon what is already known is quite common in Proverbs. We again find this same path to knowing God used by Jesus in Matthew 11:4–5. In this passage, Jesus is engaged in a conversation with emissaries from John with an important question on their minds. They want to know if Jesus is the One sent from God, whom they had been expecting. In answer to their question, Jesus said, effectively, "Look around. Take note of what you see me doing and ask yourselves if my actions fit with what you already know (from Isaiah 29:18–19) about God's Chosen One." Jesus applied the test of coherence to their quest in knowing God.

This coherence test can be quite formidable in establishing the veracity of new knowledge. When applied to knowledge of God, the drive toward making things fit into the "big picture" can result in a sense of predictability and normalcy, a feeling of trust that the Lord of all will do what is right (this is what Abraham claims in Genesis 18:25). But coherence has its limits, and all too often coherence is shattered upon the anvil of experience. Psalm 73 provides a poignant example of the crises of faith that can result when the coherence test fails and the fundamental structures thought to hold reality together break down and prove fickle. The psalmist was caught up in a dilemma: reality made sense to him, it could be counted on because he knew God was good to the upright. That is, a fundamental structure of right and wrong, reward and punishment, could be counted on because he knew God was just and acted justly. This confidence in a grand scheme of reward and punishment, right and wrong, was the argumentation also used quite effectively by Abraham in the example just cited from Genesis 18. At the heart of Abraham's dispute with God was an agreed-upon conviction, shared by both Abraham and God, that innocent people should not be punished equally with the wicked. Our psalmist, in Psalm 73, bought in to this coherent idea of right and wrong whole-heartedly and seems to have been quite content knowing how the universe worked. That was all fine and good—until his own experience made him question the validity of the coherent view of the world he had grown to rely upon (and herein was the dilemma). When his own experience made painfully clear that reward and punishment, good fortune and bad, do not follow any predictable path of morality, the psalmist was forced to admit that his coherent view of the universe required him to also conclude neither does God. The result was a crisis of faith, the complete shattering of his previously unshakable view of the universe and God. His world fell apart. Our psalmist is not alone. Similar experiences form the central thrust of Job and Ecclesiastes and inform the response offered by Jesus to his disciples when they asked, "Who sinned, this man or his parents, that he was born blind?" (John 9:1–2). When he concluded neither the blind man nor his parents, Jesus was telling his followers in no uncertain terms, "Don't put too much stock in your own designs as to how the universe should work [an over reliance upon your coherence expectations]; you may be surprised!"

Sign #3: Experience

So, information gained from reliable and trustwor-thy sources (people or sacred books) who know what they're talking about, and added to this ever-growing and strengthening coherent view of the whole (to a big picture that makes more and more sense), forms two parts of our operational triad in developing a way to know God. There is one more leg to this stool: experience. The test of experience says that knowledge about God (that is, a pathway to a God encounter) ought to be testable. If the authorities we use can be questioned by asking, *Are they reliable?* and if the coherent view of the big picture leads us to ask, *Does it make sense?* this last path to knowing God must simply inquire, *Does it work?*

This last path to knowing God is becoming more and more important to me. To explain why, I once again defer to Jesus. When his disciples asked a question very similar to what we have been considering here, Jesus' reply was pretty straightforward. His disciples were a lot like us, confused by competing claims of religious truth. They wanted to know whom to trust and what to believe. His answer: "You will know them by their fruits" (Matthew 7:16, 20; Luke 6:44). Or, in other words, he told his disciples to check them out, to test the claims and see if they work. If we attempt to apply the same test, we would need to observe the so-called authorities and see if their manner of life gives credibility to what they are telling us. We need to be willing to test our coherent view of the universe, expecting God to intrude at any time and ask, Does it make sense? And further, we need to ask one more hard question: What difference does our knowledge of God make? Or, to put it in terms similar to what Jesus used: Does time spent with God yield fruit?

The fruit can be of several kinds, but on the most fundamental level, I suggest the fruit is the way we are changed as a result of time spent with God. Does the information offered you about God resonate deeply in you, and does it lead to a sense of well-being—a contentment and peace that is not self-generated? If, indeed, we live in a created universe, and if the Creator finds pleasure in what has been created, then it seems to me that authentic and true information about the Deity will have a positive result in any of us—regardless of the religious garb in which that information is dressed. Authenticity is a good test in any interpersonal relationship, even in an interpersonal relationship with God. The authenticity of our relationship with God can be measured in the fruit it produces. Just like good friends tend to pick up each other's mannerisms and habits, time spent with God will leave a mark on any of us.

Gazing Upward

Armed with three questions—*Is it reliable? Does it make sense?* and *Does it work?*—we are ready to begin looking upward for a hole in the sky. Our exploration will begin with a consideration of the tri-faceted description of God found in the Bible. This description of God is found other places as well. As you will soon discover, the biblical description of God has been joined by layers of accumulated cultural deposits that, like the hard water deposits on water valves and faucets, needs to be chipped away if we are to really appreciate the strength of this biblical portrait. So, as we progress through the next several chapters of this book, let me encourage you to leave aside for a time the question, Is it biblical? (let's limit our religious partialities) and instead keep foremost in your thinking: Is it reliable? Does it make sense? Does it work? These three questions will guide us in our search for the hole in the sky.

PART 3
IS GOD JUST A
FOUR-LETTER WORD?

A good friend wrote to me:

> You say "God" as if that says it all. You say
> "God" with the confidence of someone who
> knows what he's talking about. Like when
> I say "pizza" or "baseball." You say "God"
> with the confidence that it will mean the
> same thing to me that it does to you. But
> I'm not so sure it does. What "God" are you
> talking about?
>
> Are you talking about the "God" that too
> many clerics use to justify their actions while

raping children? Or the "God" some clerics use to sanction *fatwas* against women who are raped by their own fathers-in-law? Or perhaps you're talking about the "God" of war and terrorism? Is it the "God" invoked to begin the chain of events on Sept. 11, 2001?

9:03 AM: Flight 175 crashes into the south World Trade Center tower.

9:28 AM: Air traffic control learns that Flight 93 has been hijacked.

9:38 AM: Flight 77 crashes into the Pentagon.

9:59 AM: The south tower of the World Trade Center collapses.

10:10 AM: Flight 93 crashes in Pennsylvania.

10:28 AM: The World Trade Center north tower collapses.

Or is it the "God" President Bush invoked right after the 9/11 attacks:

"In all that lies before us, may God grant us wisdom, and may He watch over the United States of America."

The "God" who granted him the wisdom to fight the war on terror in Iraq? I've heard "God" called upon to bring fire down upon "murdering" abortionists and "intolerant" anti-abortionists; are we talking about those "Gods"? They can't be the same one, can they? Which "God" do you mean?

My friend's challenge belongs to us all. It's easy to acknowledge someone else's "God" as a figment of their own imagination, while claiming with unwavering certainty the reality of our own "God." For those searching for a hole in the sky, this kind of self-imposed bigotry is no longer affordable. We need to face the question directly: Is "God" simply a word (four letters or not)? That's the next part of our journey.

4

Creator

Religious leaders *claim* that the bible and science harmonize completely. Scientists, not wanting to rock the boat and upset their audiences, rarely make a deliberate, concentrated effort to point out disparities between their laboratory findings and the "truth" as revealed in the Word of God.[30]

—David Mills

This chapter is the first of three that consider one of three interlocking characteristics of the Divine: Creator, Redeemer, and Lover. As we make our way through the complicated and sometimes intimidating terrain of these divine qualities, we will frequently seek direction by relying on our truth criteria established in the last chapter. All three of the God characteristics we will explore are relational: Creator, created; Redeemer, redeemed; Lover, loved. This means

---

30   David Mills, *Atheist Universe: The Thinking Person's Answer to Christian Fundamentalism* (Berkeley: Ulysses Press, 2006), 16–17.

we will be encouraged to consider God in relationship to the world around us. Sometimes that can be messy, very messy. No more so than with where we must begin: Creator.

ENTER THE CREATIONISTS AND EVOLUTIONISTS

The very first and arguably the most consistent description of God found throughout the biblical text is that of Creator. With that one description the reader of the Bible is immediately thrust into a raging twenty-first-century debate that couldn't be further removed from the way the biblical authors describe God. Both the religious leaders and the scientists, described above by David Mills, fall into the trap of thinking that the biblical references to God as Creator are intended to describe the processes that God used in creating, in a manner similar to the way those processes are described in science classes and observable through microscopes, telescopes, and all the other tools with which scientists peer into the hidden reaches of the universe. This way of reading Genesis, or any of the other biblical texts that speak of the beginnings, sets up a dichotomy between the biblical descriptions of the universe and the descriptions afforded to us by the investigations of natural science. The line of reasoning goes further and asserts that the processes at work in the universe by which the planets revolve in their orbits, plants create usable energy from sunlight, living organisms are related to one another—or any of the other physical, chemical, and biological processes and functions that can be analyzed and explained by the tools of natural science—are completely understandable by natural science, without appeal to the supernatural. Therefore, any notion of creation as described in the Bible and any designation of God as Creator is simply wrongheaded. For Mills, creationism demands evidence of the supernatural, and if "that evidence is conceded to be absent, then creationism is left with no argument at all."[31] But is the conclusion offered by Mills, and a host of likeminded scientists and religious persons (including some of the most popular religious writers in recent years: Henry Morris, Lee Strobel, and Ken Ham[32]), really so? Is the biblical description of origins akin to a scientific, albeit rather simplistic, physics or biology book? I suspect Mills would say yes. But he would be wrong.

---

31   Mills, 103.

32   Including the very popular defender of intelligent design, Lee Strobel, *The Case for a Creator: A Journalist Investigates Scientific Evidence That Points Toward God* (Grand Rapids: Zondervan, 2004) or the now somewhat out of date but still influential "creation scientists" Henry Morris and John Whitcomb, *The Genesis Flood* (Philadelphia: Presbyterian and Reformed Publishing Company, 1961). Ken Ham has become a popular author and lends his influence to the Creation Museum in Petersburg, Kentucky. Some of his many publications include *The New Answers Book* (Green Forest, AZ: Masters Books, 2006); *The Lie: Evolution* (Green Forest, AZ: Masters Books, 1987); *The Great Dinosaur Mystery Solved!* (Green Forest, AZ: Masters Books, 1998).

In all fairness to the biblical text and to those people who wrote and recorded that collection of documents, those processes so fascinating to modern scientists are of little interest to most of the biblical writers and rarely make their way into the biblical text. The description of God as Creator, when used by the biblical writers, has a focus entirely different from that in the writings of Mills, Strobel, Morris, or Ham, and the many like them. It's quite understandable that the first-time reader of the Bible gets confused. The very first page plunges us right into the middle of this modern-day conflict.

Genesis chapter 1 describes a majestic and serene cosmic progression that takes the reader on a breathtaking journey from a wild and chaotic nothingness to a fully stocked and well-running universe, all in six days and all at the behest of the Creator, who speaks everything into existence. It seems quite clear—from nothing to everything in six days—in a manner that, as Mills suggests above, is quite incompatible with the view of the universe afforded by the natural sciences. If the Genesis description is meant to offer the literary equivalent of a video recording, then there is no getting around it: Genesis and science are incompatible. Ham expresses this opinion, forcefully claiming that should this six-day creative episode in or near 4004 B.C.E. be denied, then all Christianity is forfeited.[33]

---

33   Ham, *The New Answers Book*, 105. Instead of rejecting the Genesis account, Ham opts for rejecting or revising science.

FORCING GENESIS INTO A BOX

Genesis was never intended to function like a literary video recorder, however, and Genesis 1 is not concerned with describing physical processes, telling us how the cosmos came to be. Should it be possible to travel back in time to the very beginning and observe from a quiet corner of the universe, our observations would not obviously or inevitably lead us to a description such as we find in the opening chapters of Genesis.

For the present at least, that video recording of the first moments of creation is beyond us. So if we are to test whether our Genesis 1 author intended the literary equivalent to a video recorder in what he wrote, we will need to find other means of determination. That means is available. By comparing the Genesis 1 account with other creation accounts, even from the Bible, we can determine if the Genesis 1 writer was complete in his reporting. If it can be shown that the Genesis 1 writer left important details out of the account, we will then be left with two alternatives: (1) he simply got it wrong; or (2) it must not have been his intention to provide a complete literary record of events and those left-out details are of no consequence in accomplishing his purpose.

When Genesis 1 is compared to other biblical texts referring to the Eden story, we find that the Genesis text doesn't tell all. Ezekiel offers additional details not available in Genesis. Some of those details missing in Genesis are a wealth of precious stones (Ezekiel 28:13); a mountain of God (Ezekiel 28:14); a guardian cherub in addition to the ones with flaming swords guarding the tree of life (Ezekiel 28:14); stones of fire (Ezekiel 28:16); and trees that are envious and talk (Ezekiel 31:8–9).

Given that the Genesis 1 account doesn't tell us all the available details about the Creative Event and the Garden, we must conclude either the writer of Genesis 1 botched it or that he had a different purpose in mind altogether. As we will see in a bit, the author of Genesis 1 is not sloppy or careless. Instead, the Genesis 1 text was crafted carefully, has a clear goal in mind, and is skillful in its accomplishment.

The opening chapters of the Bible are not the literary equivalent of a video recorder. Instead, the biblical descriptions are more intent on describing the *Who* of the universe. Genesis is concerned with the significance of the universe and its relationship to God and as such simply does not provide fodder for or against arguments about intelligent design, creation science, or Mills' concept of empirically defined creationism. In fact, the kinds of questions posed by Mills, Strobel, Morris, or Ham would in all likelihood seem quite absurd to the biblical writers. Grouping Genesis with a biology book or looking for physics data from Genesis makes as much sense as reading a biology book as if it were political satire or attempting to find information about loving relationships by examining the periodic table of common elements. In fact, what Mills, Strobel, Morris, and Ham fail to appreciate is how very differently the writers of the biblical texts viewed the universe around them when compared to the view common today in the modern West.

Forgive me if I appear to belabor the point. But the confusion of types of knowledge in general and confusion concerning the type of information available from books like the Bible in particular has led to unwarranted conclusions about the value of the biblical text in knowing and describing the Creator. A mistaken use of the Bible has led to a devaluation of the appropriate use of the Bible. Consequently, I believe it to be an important matter. I will use statements made by David Mills to illustrate the confusion, although similar observations could be made about those on the other side of the "creation-evolution" debate, such as Strobel, Morris, and the particularly inflammatory and often logically suspect remarks by Ham and the cohort of popular writers like him.

Mills makes a bold statement when he writes, "Genesis and the scientific method are mutually exclusive."[34] On the face of it, Mills' statement says there is no need to reconcile any fair reading of Genesis with observations coming from the modern scientific community, for Genesis and science represent two totally separate fields of enquiry. Yet, by going on to place Genesis at odds with the scientific method, Mills is actually asserting something quite different. Rather

---

34   Mills, 143.

than affirming that the Bible and science are two distinct bodies of knowledge, Mills places the two in opposition to each other and so acts as if the two (science and the Bible) are expressions of one kind of knowledge, just that one is right (science) and one wrong (the Bible).

Mills began correctly but ended incorrectly. He began by recognizing that Genesis is not a science book, in fact is mutually exclusive of science. But to then turn around and critique Genesis for being mutually exclusive of the scientific method makes as much sense as critiquing poetry for not being prose or critiquing the kind of knowledge available in legal texts for not demonstrating the emotional and intuitive sensitivity available in love sonnets. When Mills critiques the Bible for not engaging the scientific method, he is making a tragic mistake—something unwittingly done often enough. Mills goes on to explain: "Generally speaking, religious-minded individuals know little about science. And science-minded individuals know even less about the Bible."[35] But for Mills, this unfamiliarity with the Bible poses no huge obstacle, for "interpreting Scripture [I take Mills to mean Bible] is simply one person's opinion against another."[36] This reduction of Bible interpretation to opinionating certainly happens all too frequently. But I suspect Mills would want interpretations of his own writings to be governed by something other than the personal whims of

---

35   Mills, 143.

36   Mills, 144.

his readers. We should hope for the same when it comes to the Bible. But it is this reduction of Bible interpretation to opinionating that may in fact lead us to the heart of the problem and, hopefully, to a meaningful resolution.

Awareness of the kind of writing under consideration, the circumstances of the writing, and at least a working knowledge of the language in which the text was written are all helpful guides in making sense out of a book—any book, even books like the ones written by Mills and books like the Bible. These basic skills and background knowledge help the reader to keep her or his own preconceptions in check when reading and allow a meaningful exchange of information or point of view by means of the written word. Unfortunately, these basic skills and background knowledge are all but ignored when the Bible is forced into the kind of debate waged by Mills, Strobel, Morris, and Ham. The misuse of biblical languages and forms, along with ridicule heaped on top of scholars accomplished in those languages and forms, is clearly evident in the writings of Ham and is far worse than simply ignoring the biblical languages and literary forms.[37] That neglect and misuse—probably committed more frequently by religious defenders of the Bible—adds only confusion.

Imagine the horrible confusion and farfetched conclusions that would result if any of us attempted to read the front-page article of the local newspaper in the same way we read the advertisements, editorials, classifieds,

---

37   Ham, *The New Answers Book*, 94.

or comics contained in that same newspaper. Yet, we do it all the time when it comes to the Bible. Genesis 1 is a prime example. The confusion that results from ignoring literary types has been all too evident when the Genesis creation account is brought into the modern debate between creationists and evolutionists. Mills rightly considers the latest incarnation of this debate as it has coalesced around "Intelligent Design" (a way of looking at the universe affirming both the involvement of a Creator as described in Genesis 1 and the observations made by natural science) so prominently forced into the national headlines by a small town in Pennsylvania and its school board throughout the fall of 2005. Those within the camp promoting and defending Intelligent Design claim that perhaps the universe is very old and did evolve over long expanses of time, at the direction of a Creator. When reading the Genesis creation story, those in this camp tend to think of the six creative "days" followed by a seventh "day" of rest, as eons or undefined periods of time, in the same manner the word *day* is used in the phrases, "the *day* of the dinosaur" or "back in the *day*." In these two examples (and throughout Genesis chapter 1 it is argued by those of the Intelligent Design camp) "day" is not used in the narrow sense of one period of daylight separated by darkness lasting twenty-four hours. Mills rightly argues, however, that "day" (the Hebrew word is *yom*) used in Genesis 1 means just that—"day"—and that no other meaning would even be suspected had the interpreter not some outside motivation to find another meaning, as in the case with the Intelligent Design model.[38]

So both sides of the debate (the creationists and evolutionists) commit serious blunders in the way they attempt to use the very same linguistic evidence. Mills says the whole Genesis story is obviously all rubbish, because *day* means *day* and the evidence found in the cosmos around us simply can't be shoved into a single week during which everything came to be. For Mills, Genesis is plain wrong.[39] The creationists and proponents of Intelligent Design rely on the same word and insist that day must refer to a very long and sometimes indefinite age of time, and thereby concluding that Genesis is right in its description. The more radical proponents like Ham insist that *day* in Genesis chapter 1 means that twenty-four-hour period of time and, despite logical or empirical evidence to the contrary, any rejection of this understanding of Genesis 1 is tantamount to a rejection of the whole Bible![40] Both sides of the debate utilize the word "day" from Genesis chapter 1 and both sides badly misrepresent Genesis chapter 1!

---

38   Mills, 216.

39   Mills also rightly refuses to allow other somewhat ingenious explanations sometimes proposed by religious conservatives that either there was an undefined expanse of time between Genesis 1:1 and 1:2 (a gap theory) (Mills, 214) or that God created everything with the appearance of age and so the fossil record (Mills, 139). Both proposals, in my opinion, are unfortunate, making God the greatest trickster of all time.

40   Ham, *The New Answers Book*, 111-112.

Mills is right. In Genesis chapter 1, *day* means *day*, a limited amount of time usually measured from sunset to sunset. But he is flat wrong in assuming that the Genesis creation story intends to give what he and all the others in the debate label a literal accounting of how things came to be. The fact of the matter is that Genesis is much more sophisticated than that! Mills was much closer to the truth when he stated that science and Genesis 1 are mutually exclusive. The Genesis creation story is designed to give an understanding concerning the meaning of the world around us and the place of human existence within that cosmos. Any use of the account to affirm or refute a natural science description of the cosmos is plain wrong headed. Perhaps a few examples of this kind of confusion will make the matter clearer. It would be foolish to criticize the United States Declaration of Independence for not being very funny and equally foolish to believe that this critique therefore nullified the value of the document. The Declaration of Independence was never intended to be humor and so the critique is badly misplaced. Likewise, it is foolish of Mills to critique Genesis 1 for not being science and to think that somehow or other his misplaced critique diminishes the value of Genesis 1. Or, think how badly off the mark I would be should I claim that "Yabba-Dabba Do" was the root of Neanderthal linguistics because I read the phrase in a Fred Flintstone comic book. As silly as it sounds, Morris, Strobel, and particularly Ham are all attempting to do just that. They are attempting to make conclusions using linguistic evidence from Genesis 1 about topics that are totally foreign to Genesis 1. The Genesis creation story is not comedy (although many of the Bible writers use humor) nor is it a comic book, but neither is it physics, geology, or biology. None of us should be swayed by attempts to use Genesis in a way the book was never intended.

PUTTING GENESIS 1 BACK INTO ITS OWN LITERARY BASKET

Unfortunately, this kind of mixed-up use of Genesis is all too common. Is there a way out of this morass? Yes. We need to stop reading Genesis as if it were a modern-day science book. Genesis and the other biblical texts describing a creation are more at home when read alongside other "cosmological" texts, that is, texts describing the universe in broadest possible terms, including in the discussion human elements of freedom, responsibility, morality, and the like. Cosmological texts, like the one found in Genesis 1, tend to break the boundaries and mix into one grand lump what have for us come to be separate disciplines, such as physics, biology, philosophy, and religion. The result is a somewhat muddled (at least in terms of modern intellectual tastes) yet holistic mural painted in broad strokes. Cosmological texts are designed to give the reader the big picture concerning the universe and our place in it.

In the remainder of this chapter, we will explore the biblical description of God as Creator, putting that description back into its own literary basket. In our investigation we will refrain from appealing to writers and scientists such as Stephen Hawking or Albert Einstein (in the way illustrated by both Mills and Strobel, in an effort to elicit support for their respective arguments). Instead, we will make comparisons and contrasts by using fascinating writers from long ago, writers much more at home with the biblical cosmological texts (texts like Genesis 1). We will appeal to writers who communicate using the same categories of knowledge and description used by the biblical writers. Often the biblical writers are in disagreement with their contemporaries; but in using these cosmological texts from the past, we will be comparing apples with apples, unlike the practices of Mills, Strobel, Morris, and Ham.

Judging from the number and distribution of whole and partial surviving copies, one of the most popular cosmological texts from the ancient Near East is a story now called the Enuma Elish.[41] Like the Genesis creation account, the Enuma Elish presents an account of the origin of the cosmos and the divine activities that accompanied the formation of the cosmos. While the story is quite accessible and worth your while to read through it, I am providing an outline here for quick reference.

---

41   James Pritchard, *Ancient Near Eastern Texts Relating to the Old Testament* 3rd ed. (Princeton, NJ.: Princeton University Press, 1969), 60–72.

The story opens by introducing the reader to Apsu and Tiamat, the divine parents. They exist before anything else and are embodied in a flowing, undefined, and swirling mass. Apsu is given body in the primeval sweet-water ocean, Tiamat in the salt water. Their first son, Mummu, is a mist hovering over the water. Reminiscent of the Genesis creation account, all is formless and void but contains the elements from which the universe will be formed.

In time, more children are born to Apsu and Tiamat, and then grandchildren. These boisterous youngsters disturb Apsu's rest and sleep to no end. Finally, enough is enough and Apsu, along with the favored Mummu, devise a plan to destroy all the gods and so restore Apsu's longed-for peace and quiet. When Tiamat learns of this deadly plan, she is filled with grief at the prospect of losing her children and grandchildren.

One of the grandchildren, Ea, devises a plan to kill Apsu through the spell of a spoken word. After the deadly deed is done, Ea builds a spacious place to live upon Apsu's lifeless body. There, Marduk is born. Marduk is the wisest of the gods, and his skill and fame soon exalt him above all the gods.

Meanwhile, Tiamat becomes more and more disturbed over the death of her husband, Apsu. She is filled with rage and leads a rebellion, intent on killing her husband's murderers, as well as all those sympathetic with them. A devastating war between the gods looms on the horizon.

Ea, the once brave and victorious warrior, is informed of the impending peril and now mourns uncontrollably. Eventually Marduk is called upon to rescue the gods. He agrees to face Tiamat in battle, but as payment for his rescue he requires dominion over all the gods.

With great pomp and praise, Marduk prepares for the battle. As evidence of his remarkable abilities and powers he speaks a garment's destruction and its reappearance. The display of power convinces all the other gods that Marduk is a worthy leader, and he is promptly made king of the gods.

The battle between Marduk and Tiamat is enjoined with fury. Using guile as well as strength, Marduk catches Tiamat in a net. He forces a wind into her open mouth and shoots an arrow through her heart. Tiamat is dead and her body is exploded in pieces.

From Tiamat's divided body, Marduk makes two foundational parts of the universe: sky and earth. Next, Marduk creates astral stations for the great gods and organizes the calendar by setting the constellations in the sky. He fixes the sun and the moon in their courses.

Those gods who had sided with Tiamat are imprisoned and forced to serve the other gods. In short order, the menial task forced upon the imprisoned gods proves too great, so they ask Marduk for help. In response, Marduk proposes the creation of the human in order to relieve the burdens of the gods. The ring leader of the rebel gods is killed and with his blood a human is created. Humanity must now take over the work of the defeated gods and feed the host of the Babylonian deities.

Universal order and predictability in the natural world and in human society is established as the gods are organized and given specific responsibilities and duties.

While certainly the Enuma Elish and the Genesis story of creation follow distinct storylines and so are on one level quite different from each other, the Enuma Elish and the Genesis account are both of the same type of literature and so share certain characteristics. Both talk about the universe in the same general categories. Both texts use categories that combine the divine and human realms, applying the same methods of description to both. This descriptive technique makes the Enuma Elish and Genesis much more similar to one another than either is to a modern physics or geology book. Once we are able to appreciate the fact that the Enuma Elish and Genesis belong in the same literary basket—a basket quite different than the one containing physics books and geology books—we are freed from the compulsion to read either Genesis or the Enuma Elish for scientific information. This freedom allows us to read these ancient texts for what they are and so appreciate their real significance. Going even further, comparing and contrasting the two ancient texts will allow us to see the similarities and differences between them and so note what is truly remarkable and perhaps unique about each.

THE COSMOLOGY OF GENESIS

In the following few pages we will survey some of the more outstanding ideas contained in the Genesis story. We will find that the ideas in the Genesis creation story are all the more remarkable given the contrast to competing ideas from the same literary basket.[42]

The Creator Is not the Created

Perhaps it's too obvious to miss, but one of the most basic concepts found in the Genesis cosmology is an insistence on separating the created from the Creator. The Creator is not simply the sum of all that is, nor is the Creator some impersonal idea that exists as an ideal First Cause. In Genesis, the Deity expresses will, deliberates, acts upon, and makes evaluations concerning the appropriateness of the universe. There is a majestic serenity that pervades the entire episode, culminating in the final assessment that the universe is "very good." All is as it should be. Throughout the whole of chapter 1, the Genesis story makes plain that although the Creator stands apart

---

42   The interested reader may find helpful the book by John Walton, *The Lost World of Genesis One* (Downers Grove, IL: IVP, 2009).

from that which is created, the created is an expression of and bears the imprint of the Creator. Without the Creator, there would be no created. Yet, on the other hand, the universe is not some phantom that can easily be ignored. The physical universe is not inferior to the more substantive and real spiritual realities of which the physical is but a shadow on a wall. Not at all. This world we inhabit and all the sciences devoted to its exploration are real and to be taken seriously. The Creator and the created are separate from each other. The created is always susceptible to the intrusion of the Creator but the Creator is never threatened or diminished by the existence of the created. Therefore, some sort of co-opting and selective application of natural science (as practiced by Morris, reported by Strobel, or taken to extremes by Ham) in order to produce evidence for a predetermined religious outlook would find no support from the Genesis writer. But neither would the Genesis writer take seriously Mills' argument that the lack of evidence for the supernatural must lead to the conclusion that no God exists. The writer of Genesis would undoubtedly reply, in chorus with another writer, that the heavens themselves declare the glory of the Creator (Psalm 19:1). You just need to know how to look.

Mills suggests that if "the laws of physics alone do the job and perform all the work within our universe, then a Miracle Worker is left with nothing to do."[43] The writer of

---

43   Mills, 103.

Genesis 1 would be in firm disagreement, for certainly the biblical description of God's involvement with the universe makes the Deity anything but an idle observer or absent landlord. Genesis chapter 1 presents God speaking the universe into existence and then assessing that existence as good. As the chapter progresses, God speaks, makes, forms, creates, and blesses. While remaining separate from the cosmos, the Divine is actively engaged and invested in the cosmos. The repeated and summary pronouncement that "it was good" functions as a repeated declaration that the universe is just as God intended (at least as we see it at the end of Genesis 1). The natural functions and processes Mills identifies standing against the presumed supernatural evidences for the presence of a Creator are themselves presented by Genesis as the sole expression of the Creator, but in a way that prevents those processes from defining the Creator.

Oddly, the path taken by Morris, Strobel, and Ham and the path taken by Mills have much in common with the cosmology found in the Enuma Elish, and not much in common at all with the Genesis creation account. In fact, the Genesis writer would probably argue quite sternly with all four of our modern creation-evolution debaters. The Enuma Elish blurs the line between the created and the creator by capturing parts of the deities and forming them into the structures of the created universe. Some of the conquered deities are cast into the sky, forming the constellations of stars we see at night. Some of the conquered deities are slain, their blood forming the raw materials from which humans are fashioned. Morris, Ham, and Strobel blur that line between the created and the Creator by allowing only religiously vetted science to really count, thereby discounting that part of the created universe that refuses to mold itself to predetermined religious conclusions. For Morris, Ham, and Strobel, those nonconforming parts of the physical universe don't really exist. Morris, Strobel, Ham, and the writer of the Enuma Elish allow the gods in the stars to shine brightly. Mills also tends to adhere to the cosmology of the Enuma Elish by referring to a gradually disappearing "God of the gaps."[44] For Mills, "god" is what we call parts of our universe that we can't otherwise explain. As explanations are forthcoming for more and more of the universe around us, that god of the gaps shrinks ever smaller. The similarity to the Enuma Elish is quite clear. The opening scenes of the Enuma Elish take place in the celestial abode of the deities, gradually to be replaced by the more commonplace haunts of human inhabitants. As the humans assume an ever more active role, the gods fade into the background. Morris and Strobel unwittingly blur the line between the created and Creator by diminishing the reality of the physical in their efforts to conform empirical evidence to the parameters established by religious dogma. Mills blurs that same line by ignoring that which

---

44   Mills, 82–86.

may dwell beyond the physical. Mills allows existence only to that which can be empirically described and so defines the spiritual or supernatural, the Creator, out of existence. With both, the Enuma Elish would be quite pleased, but not so the writer of Genesis.

Meaning Is Possible

Having established the integrity of both the Creator and the created, the biblical authors ask the reader to consider some very fundamental characteristics of the universe we inhabit. The opening chapters of Genesis force a decision upon the reader. Either we live in a created universe or we do not. A created universe implies an intent and purpose to the whole (and its constituent parts) that has been infused from the outside by the Creator. This kind of meaning and purpose is "transcendent"; it is able to outlive any one of us and can presume a source of meaning common to all of us.

On the other hand, a universe not created—that is, a universe the product of time and chance—means there is no intent, no meaning, and no purpose other than that supplied from within, supplied by me and you. And since we are all limited to our "three score and ten," no opportunity of meaning or significance is possible beyond that brief span. So a fundamental concern of "creation" as described in

Genesis 1 is the affirmation that we live in a universe that has meaning and that, as part of that meaningful universe, we—each and every one of us—also have meaning!

Again a comparison to the Enuma Elish can be helpful. In that account of the origin, humans are granted meaning and significance in their service to the gods. Through observance of the proper ritual or sacrifice, the gods are pleased and award to the worshipper an appropriate boon, including a sense of destiny's fulfillment. But within the scope of the Enuma Elish, only a special few can repeatedly attain this plateau. The king, priest, or other privilege-born person finds an elevated status in the human realm that is mirrored in the realm of the Divine.

For the Genesis writer, all humanity has this reward. This is an amazing idea, one we still struggle with, even after all these years. The Genesis writer claims that meaning, significance, and a sense of dignity summed up in the phrase "image of God" rightly belong to all people. On the deepest level we are all equal. None of us is more important than another, and none of us can demand a higher status than another. In this regard the Genesis account is just opposite of the Enuma Elish. Genesis insists that the status and dignity assigned in the realm of the Divine is not simply a mirror of those designations in the human realm. Instead, the human realm is to be a mirror of the egalitarian status enjoyed by all in the realm of the Divine.

We Are All Connected

One of the very first characteristics of the universe that jumps out when we read the Genesis account of creation is that everything is connected. There is an organic wholeness to the Genesis description of the cosmos. Everything is interconnected and related. Everything, including us, formed from the "dust of the earth" (not far removed from Carl Sagan's description of "star stuff"[45]) finds its home within a grand latticework of interconnections, binding one to the other. There is a commonality between us more profound than the surface distinctions by which we so commonly define ourselves. Whether race, politics, national origin, or religion—despite all these markers we use to divide ourselves, we are all interrelated and the same. What happens to one of us touches us all.[46]

That message of basic human connectedness found in the Genesis story becomes even clearer when we remember the description provided in the Enuma Elish. In that account, the fundamental divisions between the gods and goddesses are reflected in fundamental divisions between people. The rifts run deep. The rift between different people provides a rationale for enslaving some, conquering others, and impoverishing even more, while a select few are

---

45   Carl Sagan, *Cosmos* (New York: Ballantine Books, 1985).

46   Even Ham and Ware have a sense of this connectedness but express it in a rather religiously polemical manner. Ken Ham and A. Charles Ware, *Darwin's Plantation: Evolution's Racist Roots* (Green Forest, AZ: Master Books, 2007).

accorded power and prestige. Genesis, on the other hand, will have none of that. In fact, a close reading of Genesis 2 shows that no such inequality is permitted—even between the sexes—for we are to one another "flesh of my flesh and bone of my bone." The Genesis writer expects that the divine values shape human social structures. At times, the notion of common human standing so clearly articulated by the writer of Genesis has been given expression in other important documents. The inspiring opening of the United States Declaration of Independence captures the vision shared by the writer of Genesis: "We hold these truths to be self-evident, that all men are created equal, that they are endowed by their Creator with certain unalienable Rights ..."

This statement calls us to rise above distinctions that divide us economically, religiously, and even nationally. But it's a call that echoes only dimly in a world increasingly filled with religious violence, economic predation, and nationalistic fervor. In order to wage war or engage in conflict with one another, we must first of all define each other as different, generally using religion, national or ethnic origin, or economic status as the fundamentals by which we divide ourselves. Genesis chapter 1 says there is a better path to follow.

CONCLUSION

So, when it comes to enlisting the influence of the Genesis cosmology, we may argue all we want about the age of the human race, wonder if an asteroid wiped out the dinosaurs, and debate what happened to all the water following a worldwide flood. We can talk about these things until we are blue in the face and totally miss the point. The biblical writers have a different focus altogether. The fact is the book of Genesis and the rest of the biblical books really don't care about the things that seem so important in the modern creation-evolution debate. Instead, the biblical writers, including the writer of the Genesis creation account, are much more interested that we affirm a fundamental solidarity, encompassing every human and leading to fair and just treatment of all.

Let me say it a little more strongly: *Incorporating the book of Genesis into religious debates about the length of a day, the age of the earth, or the absence of dinosaurs is an obscene misuse of one of the most significant documents of all time.*

We do the Genesis creation story a disservice when we value it only (or even primarily) as a source from which to mine information of the distant past. In truth, the creation story is about you and me. It is about the present. The writer of the creation story is less interested in the past than in the here and now. Adam and Eve are us. This story is our story being told in the garden. This story is, in no uncertain terms, a story of meaning, equality, and justice. It is a story that defines what it means to be human.

So what does the biblical view of Creator mean for us, you and me, people simply trying to get on in the world? Most fundamentally it means that we are not alone in the universe. There is a Creator who takes pleasure in what he has made. Like it or not, our very existence means that we are forever and inescapably invested with meaning and significance by the One who made us. Each and every one of us is important to at least one Person—to the one Person whose opinion really matters.

Recognition of the Creator is only the beginning of the story, however. A serious acceptance of the relationship we have with the Creator soon gives birth to sober questions, not the least of which is this: Couldn't the Creator have done a better job of it? Despite the wonderful descriptions of a "very good" universe in Genesis 1, I think it would be pitifully naive if any of us attempted that same evaluation of the world we inhabit. If "Creator" is the sole description of God available to us from the biblical text, then I, for one, have some serious questions to ask, because I'm not sure he did that great a job. I'm not the only one with questions. The biblical writers, too, are dissatisfied with leaving our understanding of God wrapped up in this one descriptive term, Creator. To it they quickly add two other terms that form an amazing triad capable of carrying us through the whole of the biblical drama. This triad can be used to form one sentence, capturing the essence of the Bible's description of the hole in the sky: *I was created by God to be loved and redeemed by God.* Lover and Redeemer must now be explored in our search for God.

5

Redeemer

The word *redeemer*, when used to describe God, can easily become overly religious. Don't get me wrong, though. Simply being religious doesn't make the word bad. And the word does have a long history of beneficial use, including use by many of the biblical writers. It's just that this perfectly fine word has dropped out of common, ordinary conversation and when it is used, it conjures up images in stained glass or a picture of Jesus with a little lamb cradled in his arms. For many, the word doesn't have immediate application to real, everyday life, and so its use in describing God has the effect of shoving God off to a corner in some church somewhere.

Despite the fact that the word itself has dropped out of favor, the idea about God that the word *redeemer* was intended to communicate, at least by the biblical writers, remains valuable. In a nutshell, when applied to God, "Redeemer" means that God will and is now actively engaged in making everything right. Usually, when used in the Bible, the word describes the process of buying something back or restoring something to its former preferred status. A possession, field, or person once pawned off for some reason or other can be redeemed, or bought back, and so restored to its original condition. In its broadest scope, the redeeming God is said to be engaged in restoring all of creation, and people in particular, to an original state of goodness described in Genesis 1–2. In other words, God is making things right again.

Perhaps one of the most powerful stories illustrating this idea of redemption is found in the book of Hosea. This little prophetic book uses the story of Hosea's troubled marriage to the prostitute and unrepentantly promiscuous Gomer as an illustration of how Israel has strayed from her "marriage" to God. Two children born to Hosea and Gomer are oddly named: Lo-ruhamah (Not pitied) and Lo-ammi (Not my people) (Hosea 1:6, 9). These names are intended to describe the totally broken relationship and thoroughly hopeless condition in which God's wayward people now find themselves. The break is total. It is thorough. And it is beyond the repair of the Israelites themselves. Yet, the story moves on. The amazing drama of redemption will not allow this condition to persist. These two unfortunate children, Lo-ruhamah and Lo-ammi, are redeemed, restored, and renamed. "Not pitied" becomes "Pitied" and "Not my people" becomes "My people" (2:23). By means of this name change, we are told something of the scope of redemption. The broken condition is changed entirely. The redemptive activity of God is just as total and thorough as the need—and more. The broken are repaired and the hopeless are filled with hope. This isn't just window dressing or a fresh coat of paint covering hidden imperfections. No, God's redemption is complete, working from the inside out and thoroughly remaking the redeemed, undoing the previous wrong, recreating, and making things right again.

The "making things right again" sense of the word *redeemer* lies all too often in stark contrast to the limited scope of the currently favored religious use of the word. In most religious contexts *redeem* refers primarily or even exclusively to God's activity that saves my soul when I die, granting me an eternal life in heaven where all is happy and peaceful. I find this description of heavenly bliss very appealing, but it only begins to capture the breadth of God's redeeming activity described in the Bible. The writers of the Bible present a redeeming God who is making all things right, not just giving me entrance to heaven when I die. It isn't just my soul that is being bought back and restored, but me—all of me! My hopes and dreams, my fears and regrets. Those horrific experiences and devastating losses we all experience. All the wrongs I have endured and forced others to endure. All of it is being redeemed. All of me is being made right! The redeeming God is now engaged in and will at some point complete my total restoration. Everything will be made right.

As you might suspect, this total, redeemed restoration means that the biblical description of God as Redeemer is big—very, very big. Not only is all creation caught up in

redemption's net, but so, too, is all history. I don't pretend to
know how it works, but it is clear that, in the Bible at least,
the concepts of redemption and creation, when applied to
God, go hand in hand. Redemption is as big as all creation,
and creation itself is an act of redemption. But there's more.
In the Bible, God's redeeming efforts rarely stay confined
to the present. Those efforts have a way of reaching both
into the distant future and into the distant past. Redemption
becomes, for those convinced of its ultimate fruition, a hope
and a way of living that, as we will see in a little bit, has
drastic consequences in the here and now. But redemption also provides, once again for those convinced of its
ultimate completion, a comfort and rest when looking back
into the past. When subjected to redemption, the past is
not a closed book, unalterably finished and complete. In
God's redemptive scheme, history works backward. The
future completion of the redemptive process is a surety
that seeps backward through all time, changing the present
and rewriting the past. In God's redemptive scheme tears
are wiped away, and pain, grief, and sorrow are all turned
inside out, becoming occasions for joy and laughter. This
is the good news of the redeeming God!

But is it so? Can this picture of the redeeming God—
as big as all creation and never owned or tamed by the
self-interests of any one religious group—really be true?
I'll admit, I can easily become overwhelmed by the sheer
excitement of the Bible's portrait of the redeeming God.

Still, I recognize that while God's redeeming work is a plan put in progress (with no threat of stalling), it is nevertheless not yet a completed fact. Redemption requires that we must live in anticipation of the time when joy is full. So the question becomes: While we now reside in this betwixt and between state, is there any evidence or assurance that all this talk of a redeeming God is something more than so much fantasy borne out of insecurity or despair? Perhaps. Let's return to our three knowledge criteria of authority, coherence, and experience and see where they lead us.

AUTHORITY: IS IT RELIABLE?

Is the biblical descriptive of God as Redeemer reliable? Let's start this part of the investigation in a very broad sense and ask: Is the redeeming God a claim made with consistency by witnesses whose testimony is credible? Surveying the consistency of the claim is the easy part. Determining the credibility of those witnesses is a bit more difficult. In the following survey we will attempt to establish reasonable controls regarding the testimony we will accept as valid. We will consider credible testimony made by individuals (1) at great personal risk or cost, (2) accompanied by behavioral changes relative to the claim of redemption, and whose testimony, if believed, (3) has similar life-changing potential for others, transferring to these other people a witness of the same redemption.

This list of criteria will help us identify witnesses who believe their own testimony and demonstrate firsthand the changing power of the claim they make. With this list of criteria, I'm not suggesting that only those meeting this standard can experience the redemptive power of God or give evidence of that redemption. No, not at all. The criteria simply attempt to establish a high threshold that eliminates witnesses of mixed motivation. Consequently, if it can be shown that someone, by making the claim of God as Redeemer, stands to benefit financially, socially, or in some other immediate fashion, his or her claim will not be accepted as credible. Neither will we accept the claims made by those with martyr complexes, regardless of the attractiveness of those claims, for those claims do not pass the test of transferability. So, armed with our three tests for credibility, we will survey the Bible to find if there is a consistent testimony made by credible witnesses. If found, that testimony will serve as a reliable authority statement, giving witness to the redemption by God.

Testing the Bible's Claim

The claim of divine redemption is consistently made in the Bible, and those attesting to the redemptive power of God are numerous, as we might expect. After all, one of the chief reasons these particular books were collected into the Bible is because of their redemptive proclamation. And so we could be forgiven for thinking that perhaps the Bible is not a very suitable place to look for objective testimony. But when we begin to examine the credibility of those witnesses using the three qualifying criteria we established above, a very interesting chain of testimony begins to show itself across the biblical record.

The call of Abraham (Abram) in Genesis 12:1–3 appears early in the biblical record and fits our test of credibility. Abraham is asked to risk everything by moving to a strange, unidentified land. Genesis 12:4 indicates that Abraham complied with this divine order in a simple and straightforward manner: "So Abram went, as the LORD had told him." True, Abraham is offered a tempting benefit in the form of a future divine blessing that holds forth the promise of numerous descendants. A blessing that, as the story unfolds, becomes more and more doubtful and finally downright absurd, as Abraham and his wife Sarah remain childless well into their senior years. Then, this same blessing is placed at great risk by the seemingly fickle and abhorrent divine demand that would threaten to take the life of Abraham's son (Genesis 22). Thus, as a motivator for Abraham's action, this future promise of descendants seems a very tenuous promise at best. Instead, the bottom line describing Abraham's response to God in Genesis 12 is a benefit made available to "all the families of the earth" (verse 3) through Abraham's participation in the divine redemptive plan. Later writers look back on this figure from the earliest part of the biblical redemption story and identify him as a model and exemplar in no small measure because of his trust in the redemptive God without the benefit of immediate reward.

We could add to Abraham's testimony those given by Moses, Jeremiah, Paul and Jesus himself. All fit our tests for credibility. In fact, this is exactly what one writer of the New Testament does and more. In chapter 11, the writer of Hebrews provides example after example of people who suffer abuse and mistreatment without reward because of their persistent faith in the divine redemptive plan, as they understood it. Each experienced a fundamental change because of his or her participation in that redemptive power, and each recommended the same to others. Receiving the testimony from people of the past, the writer of Hebrews turns and commends the redeeming God to others: "Therefore, since we are surrounded by so great a cloud of witnesses, let us also lay aside every weight" (Hebrews 12:1).

The point is the Bible provides a chain of witnesses, all of whom experienced significant upheavals in their personal circumstances, usually at great cost, because of their encounter with a divine redemptive event. As a consequence of their experience, these people felt compelled to recommend to others participation in that same divine redemption.

Found Beyond the Bible

This type of testimony isn't limited to stories from the Bible. For many, the witness of experience remains the strongest evidence to redemption's power. Conversion stories, describing an immoral or tragic life prior to a conversion or "born again" experience can be traced back to the early Puritan movement and are now commonplace in evangelical forms of Christianity. But witnesses to redemption's scheme are much broader than this one religious form, and in fact may be most compelling when shed of their exclusively religious garb. Eulogies and memorials during Ted Kennedy's funeral services frequently included passionate gratitude for the senator's tireless work on behalf of the disadvantaged and a promise for more to come, even as the senator, himself, now enjoys a fuller experience of his own redemption. The public memorial in Boston drew long lines of the disenfranchised and those who, time after time, expressed gratitude for the manner in which Senator Kennedy gave a voice to the voiceless. Redemption's most powerful witness is seen in action, not just heard in words. Perhaps this is what the writer of James was getting at when he held treatment of widows and orphans as a visible measure of "pure and undefiled" religion (1:27).

Some time ago I shared a classroom with a young man from Somalia. He was a refugee, recently immigrated to the United States, weaving together a life from threads that most of us take for granted. Occasionally, he would talk to the rest of the class about his experience. He spoke about walking hundreds of miles with surviving members of his family to escape the violence threatening to rob every shred of life and hope. His stories of danger and escape, the overwhelming sensory assault that greeted him in the large cities of Europe and North America, and the constant newness of every day were spellbinding. What I remember most was the way his eyes would shine when he described his new life. He was so happy to be sitting in a college classroom and found joy all around him. The first day it snowed that semester, the whole class revolted, and eighty or so people ran outside and placed him into the middle of a wild and chaotic snowball fight. I can still see his unbounded joy rippling over that whole group until everyone was caught in its giddy grip. He was always quick to describe his experience as a redemptive gift given from the hand of God. Even though he and I do not share the same religious tradition, his descriptions resonated with my own experiences of sharing in that mighty redemptive stream. All of us could be happy with him.

But what about all those people who never survived the long walk to freedom? What about the people caught in the cauldron of war and terror who don't live to tell the tale? Is there no redemption for them? I have a friend who serves as chaplain in one of our local hospitals. He willingly walks with people through dark days. He sits with people during long hours of surgery and is often there when emergencies are taking place. Usually, the pain and fright accompanying the illness or trauma experienced by a loved one—or worse, those without family or friends—is overcome as health is restored. Sometimes, however, there is no restoration, and the hospital room becomes a sacred place for final goodbyes. Where is redemption then? Oddly, my chaplain friend confesses it's in these moments that redemption is time and again most clearly seen. Redemption is seen in the hope that lifts the fallen and grieving. Redemption is seen in the conviction that the story is not finished and that a future is secure—even during a tearful goodbye.

For all of us, the persistent press of stories that don't turn out well is a constant reminder that Redemption's work is not complete and hope is needed. Hope, however, can often slip into fantasy and escape. So now we must ask ourselves: Does this incomplete nature of redemption mean it has serious flaws that threaten its very credibility? It's a good question.

COHERENCE: DOES IT MAKE SENSE?

Moving to the second of our criteria for testing the truth claim of divine redemption, let's consider if the claim is coherent, or makes sense. Once again, we'll start our inquiry by stepping far back and asking in the broadest possible terms: Is the idea of redemption itself coherent? When we move back to gain this broad perspective, one thing becomes very striking: every religious tradition affirms redemption in some form or other. Certainly, the major religions of the West and all their many permutations advocate some form of redemptive plan. The same is true of the traditionally Eastern religions. Even those religious traditions preferring a reincarnated life experience do so in order to purge that life experience from destructive aspects and influences, thus redeeming life itself. Redemptive themes aren't limited to religious traditions. Even nihilism—the idea that all is chaos and meaningless—tends toward the redemptive, banishing evil from existence. The point is redemption (the movement toward the good) is recognized by practically all religious and philosophical systems. What could possibly explain this seemingly ubiquitous presence of a redemptive component as part and parcel of the way the majority of humanity has always sought to make sense out of life? Could it be that buried somewhere deep in the human heart is an awareness that something isn't quite right, a longing for a better and more perfect existence?

The redemptive theme is certainly foundational to the biblical view of reality. In fact, the claim of God as Redeemer is a linchpin that makes the rest of the biblical view of reality coherent. The biblical writers see redemption in a broad scope connecting and intertwining the theme with creation. The theme of redemption is introduced in the Bible's description of beginnings. The well-ordered and "very good" creation of Genesis 1:31 is disrupted and spoiled through the actions of the human inhabitants. They are removed from the Garden of Bliss and wander in a reality characterized, like ours, by harm, fear, pain, and death. But hope is not abandoned, for a persistent thread running through the whole story is a redemption—a buying back to restore the initial goodness of creation. This hope gives rise to the promise made to Abraham, a promise that, as we saw earlier, encompasses all humanity in its embrace. This grand design is maintained to the very end of the biblical story in which redemption is often characterized as a creation of a "new heaven and a new earth."

> Then I saw a new heaven and a new earth;
> for the first heaven and the first earth had
> passed away, and the sea was no more. And
> I saw the holy city, the new Jerusalem, com-
> ing down out of heaven from God, prepared
> as a bride adorned for her husband. And I
> heard a loud voice from the throne saying,
>
> "See, the home of God is among mortals.
> He will dwell with them;
> they will be his peoples,
> and God himself will be with them;

> he will wipe every tear from their eyes.
> Death will be no more;
> mourning and crying and pain will be no
> more,
> for the first things have passed away.'
> And the one who was seated on the throne
> said, "See, I am making all things new."
> (Revelation 21:1–5 NRSV)

Reality, as we know it, is created and the object of redemption. Because redemption is connected to the broadness of creation, redemption can never become the sole possession of any particular group or ideology. Redemption, at least as it is presented in the Bible, is much too big for any of us to own. Yet, this very thing has been attempted time and again.

Co-opting Coherence

The coherence of the biblical presentation of the redeeming God breaks down when redemption is co-opted to become the private domain of a particular religious or ethnic group. Our introduction to Abraham (Abram) back in Genesis 12 points us beyond the particular of Abraham and his descendants to the general and universal, indicating that the real goal of God's choice of Abraham is to effect a positive benefit available to "all the families of the earth"

(Genesis 12:3). In like manner, the Hebrew prophets of the Old Testament point Israel beyond herself to a consideration of God as sovereign over all nations and actively engaged in the redemption of all peoples—even those who oppose Israel (Isaiah 19:24–25)! Jesus and several writers of the New Testament continue this chorus sung powerfully by the prophets. Jesus spoke of a redemption available to all people (Matthew 8:11), offered to those who need it most: "Come to me, all you that are weary and are carrying heavy burdens, and I will give you rest. Take my yoke upon you, and learn from me; for I am gentle and humble in heart, and you will find rest for your souls" (Matthew 11:28–29 NRSV).

Paul was convinced that ethnic origin, race, gender, economic status, or even religion itself could prove no effective barrier to the redeeming activity of God (Romans 3:29; 9:24; Galatians 3:8, 14, 28).

Yet, time and again, this great gift from the redeeming God has been hoarded and used in an attempt to elevate one person or group over others. This self-serving caricature of the redeeming God may indeed fail the test of coherence. But the failure of the caricature can never diminish the wonder of the Real.

EXPERIENCE: DOES IT WORK?

The final hurdle in testing the truth claim of divine redemption is simply this: Does the descriptive of God as

Redeemer work? Does God actually redeem, and does that redeeming activity have a positive effect on those being redeemed? If redemption is perceived as entrance into heaven when I die, then except for the occasional—and in my opinion, spurious—claims by those who allege to have been there and come back, there can be no firsthand witness to redemption. If, however, redemption is the process initiated by God to make all things right, culminating in a renewed life in heaven, then there ought to be ample, indeed, abundant evidence in the form of experience. In fact, if the divine redemptive claim has no experiential evidence, then I would be the first to admit the claim is useless.

Although imperfectly and incompletely, I've experienced the divine redemptive claims to be true. Though the inconsistency of my own experience is a cause of frustration, I must also recognize that I'm not the only one who has ever felt this way. The writer or Romans 8 expressed the frustration more eloquently than I ever could:

> For the creation waits with eager longing for the revealing of the children of God; for the creation was subjected to futility, not of its own will but by the will of the one who subjected it, in hope that the creation itself will be set free from its bondage to decay and will obtain the freedom of the glory of

the children of God. We know that the whole creation has been groaning in labor pains until now; and not only the creation, but we ourselves, who have the first fruits of the Spirit, groan inwardly while we wait for adoption, the redemption of our bodies. For in hope we were saved. Now hope that is seen is not hope. For who hopes for what is seen? But if we hope for what we do not see, we wait for it with patience. (Romans 8:19–25 NRSV)

In this writer's view, there is evidence all around us that redemption's plan has begun, is steadily progressing, but has not yet reached completion. The incomplete nature of redemption's work creates a tension within those eager to experience the fullness of redemption's end. Could it be that this tension is part of the experiential evidence confirming the reality of the redeeming Divine? Does the heartbreak lovers experience during separation provide confirming evidence for the depth of their love in the same way that believers long for redemption's final act?

But we should not get the idea that we experience redemption only through its absence. Powerfully, I've seen redemption's confirming peace firsthand. While in the midst of a serious and life-threatening medical condition, my wife was able to share with me her own witness to the reality of redemption's plan by recounting to me what she called her "keyhole moments." These keyhole moments were times of unrepentant and untamed joy that captured her, independent of any visible or otherwise discernable source. These moments, she explained, were a result of glimpses caught as she peered through the keyhole of heaven's door and witnessed redemption's fullness that waited for her. Obviously, her descriptions of these glimpses were metaphorical and the joy she experienced was the result of having been captured by the reality of redemption's goal. Redemption's goal reordered her perception of everything else and expressed itself in joy. I, too, have had these "keyhole moments" and have found them to be unplanned, uncontrolled, and much too infrequent. One particularly memorable encounter left me with no better description than to simply say, "God tucked me in." The experience left me with an undeniable and tangible sense of well-being, the same a child would get when being put to bed at night by a loving parent.

But there are other and no less shocking ways in which redemption is experienced. The writer of Romans 12 encouraged his readers to think differently, to think with redemption in mind. He went on to describe the result of this shift in thinking as nothing less than a total transformation (Romans 12:2), an observable behavioral change. According to this writer, the reality of redemption is available to experience now.

The writer of Romans 12 has extended to us a challenge. Give it a try. See if it works with the very next person you see, or even the next time you look into a mirror. When that person comes into view, or the reflection in the mirror greets you, think of that person first and foremost as an object of redemption, in the process of being remade and the recipient of unbounded divine love. In other words, transform your thinking in the manner recommended by the writer of Romans 12. If you do, and if Romans 12 has merit to it, you should find a self-confirming joy that reinforces the correctness of your new perception. Peace, joy, and love, in tangible measure, provide the experiential criteria confirming the reality of redemption.

In my mind, the most astounding and concise explanation of the behavioral changes that occur when redemption is experienced is found in arguably the most famous part of the New Testament: Matthew 5–7, the Sermon on the Mount. In these three short chapters, the teaching of Jesus is condensed into a hard-hitting and truly remarkable sermon. In the sermon, Jesus advocates for an extensive moral transformation that effectively turns typical priorities and values on their heads. Those who mourn, the poor, the meek, the persecuted, and peacemakers are all congratulated, for the kingdom of heaven (the fullness of redemption) awaits them. In Jesus' portrayal, redemption's goal seeps backward through time and provides the basis for remarkable behavioral changes now. The point being, for us at this moment, *the most powerful experiential evidence for the redeeming Divine is the unexpected and otherwise unexplained changes overcoming people who, contrary to their own immediate best interests, value others ahead of themselves and are willing to forgo self-advancement in pursuit of the kingdom of heaven.* Like that proverbial "pearl of great price" or that "glimpse through the keyhole," something is out there that demands our attention and ambitions. That "something" is the redeeming Divine.

WHERE THE RUBBER MEETS THE ROAD

It is one thing to speak of the grand scope of redemption and God's concern for all history. It is another thing altogether to see redemption at work in the immediate and individual. In some ways, it's easier to think about and accept the big picture. But when two young children lose their parents in a tragic house fire, or a marriage falls apart with all the dashed hopes and dreams that marriage promised, or a job loss forces a home foreclosure—where is redemption's plan then? Can these behavior changes we read about in the Sermon on the Mount be evidenced even in the ugly side of life? Yes, I think so, and that is where our journey must take us next.

Before we begin this discussion, however, let's consider how we ought to think about this together. Personal tragedy is real, and, in my opinion, any attempt to parade it about simply to make a point is despicable. I don't want to do that here. I realize it has become fashionable in some religious settings to single out people in distress, bringing the person onstage so they may tell the group their tragic story and how the religious group played a central role in bringing about a remedy. In such instances, the tragedy becomes an advertisement for the merits of the group. I don't think we ought to use each other in that manner. In my experience at least, the redemption of personal tragedy rarely seeks a stage, is generally quiet, and is always humble. The redemption of personal tragedy may not resolve or remove the tragedy and the accompanying pain. Therefore, I want to step lightly. I want to think with you about the promise of redemption even in the face of the pain we must all endure, but as a fellow sufferer, with questions of my own. The essence of the Christian message is this: *Life from a reality unseen suffered death in the reality seen so that death in the reality seen could never assail life in that reality unseen.* Motivating this cosmic redemptive exchange is divine love, and that's the next part of our journey.

6

Lover

I recently read an article written by a prominent American theologian nearing the end of his career. The article was an honest and authentic attempt to describe the faith of a theologian by a person well versed in both the advantages and pitfalls of religious professionalism. While there was much in the article I found helpful, I must admit that in the end, the article left me hollow and empty. I felt empty because throughout, faith is described as an intellectual assent to a set of beliefs or way of looking at life that fits into the grand scheme of a particular religious outlook. Faith, according to this article, is a way of thinking that accepts a particular definition of "truth" approved by a set of religious authorities. Although they would disagree with the particular brand of "truth" affirmed by the theologian who wrote this article, many religious leaders and theologians, from a variety of religious traditions, see faith in the same way—as something to know just like biology, history, or the names of the neighborhood kids.

In my opinion, "faith" defined as knowledge of the right set of beliefs and doctrines falls short and misses the point. I'm not alone in my disagreement. The books of the Bible present faith as a multifaceted human experience. The Old Testament does not have just one word that can be translated "faith" but instead uses a whole range of terms, which, taken together, imply faith is an event or encounter, not just intellectual agreement. The New Testament writers, firmly rooted in the Hebrew way of looking at faith as an encounter, add to the experiential understanding of faith by emphasizing and more specifically defining the object of the faith encounter. This should be expected since, as a minority within the larger Judaism, the followers of Jesus struggled to express how the life, death, and resurrection of Jesus impacted their encounter with God. The testimony of the biblical writers is that faith is an attitude of trust and disposition of reliance on the object of faith. To be sure, the trust and reliance in which faith expresses itself involves knowing some things about the object of faith, but that knowledge alone is only a prelude to faith, not faith itself. I would be the first to agree that there are things about God that can be known in the same way we know biology, history, or the names of the neighborhood kids, but there is more. Knowing the names of those kids isn't the same as knowing the kids, and knowing things about God isn't the same as knowing God. The biblical triad describing God—Creator, Redeemer, and Lover—is a description of a Person, not a way of describing a set of beliefs or doctrines. The God who loves us is known best by trust, not by our ability to recite the right creed.

THE NATURE OF THE EVIDENCE

The previous two descriptions of God—Creator and Redeemer—describe actions God takes on behalf of others. Those actions can be observed and leave tangible evidence. God as Lover, however, intends to describe an attitude or disposition that God has toward us and is not limited to any specific action. So the question is: What evidence do we look for to show an attitude or disposition? Perhaps we ought to apply the same tests we would use to measure the authenticity of any loving relationship. There are three:

1. The testimony of the one loved: "I feel that I am loved because ..."
2. The testimony of the one loving: "I love this person because ... And I show it in ..."
3. Observation by a third party: "God must really love you because I observe ..."

None of the three statements have only one right completion. Each statement is best filled out when it is individualized and written in a manner that fits the needs, interests, and personality of the parties involved. For example, a rafting trip together with one of my children might well be an act of love but would turn into an act of cruelty and meanness if I knew that child feared the water. What qualifies as an act of love to one person may be anything but to somebody else! So, in using the three vantage points from above (the Lover, the loved, and the third-party observer), we will need to triangulate and look for places where the testimonies from all three converge in order to best understand this descriptive of God as Lover.

The Loved

Let's first consider the testimony of the one loved: me and you. And, let's begin backward by considering first the result when love is absent. Why is it that all of us function better when we are loved? I have a friend who, when his job requires him to act in a manner that disappoints or angers others, will often vent to me by quoting lines from a movie: "All I want is to be loved! Is that so wrong!?" Truth be told, that's all any of us want. Why is that? Why is it we are happier, function better, and seem more content when we are loved? Could it be that we were created to be loved? Could it be that the Creator deeply loves what he has created and fashioned each of us to find joy in the love he has for us? Could it be that all the loves we enjoy and desire are but pointers directing us to Love itself?

This one common desire for love is found in just about every religious tradition (and nonreligious traditions as well). When people attempt to explain or describe the human place in the universe, most will express their own unique take on this one common theme of love. Whether it's "being at one with the universe," "experiencing dependency on the Absolute," "living in peace and harmony" with what is, or "letting the Force flow through you," all are struggling to express this commonly felt need to be loved. If our partner in this cosmic love affair is impersonal—a force or Absolute—then we are left with a sense of harmony and oneness with what is. As soon as this great Absolute assumes characteristics of personality, then our need for oneness and harmony becomes a search for love. Why is that? Given the vast differences among us, the wide range of likes and dislikes, the intense variety by which we attempt to structure our lives, why is it we all want to be loved? And is this so wrong? The biblical tradition answers this question by simply observing it's because the Creator wants to love us. We have a need to be loved because the Creator has a desire to love and so created us with a bent to respond to absolute love. So, what about testimony from the one loved? If it's at all true that the acknowledgment from the divine Lover is "I created you and redeemed you because I love you," what about you and me? How does the one loved amass evidence of being loved by the divine Lover?

In broad strokes encompassing the very personal, individual, and sometimes unique experiences of being loved by the Creator, the biblical writers describe the experience of that divine love as a sense of well-being, completeness, and wholeness. Surrounded by the love of the Creator, we, the loved and created, find security and peace. The Creator's love produces a sense of "rightness" that nothing can disturb. One writer expressed this well-being: "But I am like a green olive tree in the house of God. I trust in the steadfast love of God for ever and ever" (Psalm 52:8).

Confidence in God's love led to a sense of well-being likened to that seen in a healthy, green olive tree rooted and thriving in a place of peace and quietness. While there may be similarity in the end result of love, the way we all get there isn't the same. The Creator's desire to love and our need to be loved doesn't mean that all our experiences of love are identical. Love is one of those human interactions that, when most authentic, is also most personal. Love doesn't fit into a box and often makes up its own rules as it goes along. My experience can't be used as a test by which to measure yours, and your experience can't be used as a norm by which to mold mine. Yet, there are enough commonalities in what we experience as love to allow us conversation and mutual understanding when we think together about our experiences of love. Some of those commonly experienced aspects of love with the

Creator have been written about by the biblical writers and deserve our attention.

One of those biblical writers used his understanding of the death and resurrection of Jesus as evidence of God's love.

> What then are we to say about these things? If God is for us, who is against us? He who did not withhold his own Son, but gave him up for all of us, will he not with him also give us everything else? Who will bring any charge against God's elect? It is God who justifies. Who is to condemn? It is Christ Jesus, who died, yes, who was raised, who is at the right hand of God, who indeed intercedes for us. Who will separate us from the love of Christ? Will hardship, or distress, or persecution, or famine, or nakedness, or peril, or sword? As it is written, "For your sake we are being killed all day long; we are accounted as sheep to be slaughtered." No, in all these things we are more than conquerors through him who loved us. For I am convinced that neither death, nor life, nor angels, nor rulers, nor things present, nor things to come, nor powers, nor height, nor depth, nor anything else in all creation,

will be able to separate us from the love
of God in Christ Jesus our Lord. (Romans
8:31–39 NRSV)

This is an amazing set of sentences! It is significant to
note that, according to the writer of Romans 8, this one
supreme act of love invalidates all our attempts to find
evidence of God's love in other places. This is an unusual
idea, not at all popular in modern evangelical Christianity.
Television and radio airwaves as well as Christian bookstore
shelves are full of advice that directs us to an experience
of the love of God in financial prosperity, physical health,
and relational tranquility. God's love is said to be evident
in large church buildings full of happy people and large
bank accounts, whose smiling pastors can successfully
lead others to experience the fullness of God's love as
well. (Think of the pressure that puts on those people!)
The writer of Romans 8 will have none of this. According
to our writer, the difficulties in life (hardship, distress, per-
secution, famine, etc.) are incapable of negating evidence
of God's love; and so, presumably, the inverse of those
difficulties (wealth, good health, social esteem, etc.) are
equally incapable of providing additional verification of
God's love. Everything else (money, esteem, health, or
apparent religious success) pales into insignificance when
compared to the death and resurrection of Jesus as evidence for God's overpowering love for us.

How can this be? How can it be that absolutely nothing in the whole universe is capable of separating us from the love of God?! Isn't this simply a flight of fancy that seeks escape from the reality of horror and tragedy visiting us all? I think we must conclude the writer of Romans 8 more than a little off base if not for the purpose of the loving act he observes in the death and resurrection of Jesus. The love of God takes form in the redemptive acts of God, of which the death and resurrection of Jesus is supreme and culminating. So expansive is God's redemptive act that the universe itself is caught in its web, subject to the love of God and so susceptible to redemption no less than us, its inhabitants! Therefore, all we experience—the good and the bad—is transformed by redemption's love and can neither add to nor detract from that love. And notice our recognition of the love seems to add little, if anything, to God's love for us.

This same sentiment as that found in Romans 8 was expressed more simply in the oft memorized "For God so loved the world that he gave his only begotten Son" (John 3:16).

If we need to look for evidence that God loves us, no better can be found than in the gift of the Son. So, is there evidence that we are loved by God? Yes. Love that redeems all else is wrapped up in the death and resurrection of Jesus.

The Lover

Let's now turn to the testimony of the divine Lover. How would God complete the following: "I love this person because … and show it in …"? Admittedly, we are limited in our search for evidence to what others have written about the Divine, submitting those statements to the tests of coherence and experience. But even given the circumspect nature of the evidence available, evidence does exist.

The Bible will function as our sourcebook for this circumspect evidence. But, don't think that by looking in the Bible for evidence of the Divine's disposition of love that we are stacking the deck by looking in a book predisposed to prove that love. Some of the strongest protests and pleas stemming from the felt absence of the divine love come from the Bible, and it's to these that we must turn first.

The book of Job is in many ways a protest against the absence of the divine love. The main character of the book is robbed of all life's blessings and so is forced to reassess his notion that those good things in life are foolproof evidence of divine favor and love. Job expresses confusion over the apparent erratic nature in the way God has recently treated him. He is confused because God's maltreatment is at odds with the very fact of creation. Job asks of God, "Does it seem good to thee to oppress, to despise the work of thy hands …?" (Job 10:3), and out of exasperation and utter disbelief complains, "Thy hands fashioned and made me; and now thou dost turn about and destroy me.…Thou hast granted me life and steadfast love" (Job 10:8, 12). Underlying Job's confusion is a belief that the very fact of creation is an evidence of God's love. Job exists. That alone is evidence that he is loved by God. For, in Job's mind, creation is not a dispassionate act of the Creator but an act motivated by desire for the created. Job later contemplates his own disappearance into nonexistence and concludes, "Thou wouldst call, and I would answer thee; thou wouldst long for the work of thy hands" (Job 14:15). Should Job begin down a path leading to his own nothingness, God would call him back, for God longs for the work of his hands. In other words, Job's disappearance would be God's eternal loss, for God loves his creation.

Job isn't the only book in the Bible to make this connection between creation and love. Ezekiel repeatedly makes the claim that God has no pleasure in the death of anyone (18:32), not even the wicked (18:23; 33:11), and so agrees with Job that God longs for the work of his hands. The psalms reinforce this idea but apply the divine desire only to his people (147:11; 149:4). Even if reluctant and contrary, the people of God cannot escape the Creator's love (Jeremiah 31:31–34) but will once again pick up the chorus:

> Give thanks to the LORD of hosts,
> For the LORD is good,
> For his steadfast love endures for ever!
> (Jeremiah 33:11)

The wonder and amazement of the biblical story is that, after describing the full extent of God's love by applying that love to his special people, the biblical drama turns right around and claims all people are God's special people! All people, even Israel's mortal enemies, are God's special people and the work of his hands: "Blessed be Egypt my people, and Assyria the work of my hands, and Israel my heritage" (Isaiah 19:25).

This prophetic vision of all people as recipients of divine love, simply by virtue of having been created by God, reinforces the evaluation made in the very opening pages of the Bible. The repeated divine assessment made after every creative act—"it was good"—is culminated after the creation of the human with God's pronouncement that it is now "very good!" This evaluation isn't made by judging the creation against some cosmic yardstick to see if it is poor, so-so, good, or very good. No, the divine pronouncement is made by comparing the fact of creation with the divine intent of creation. In other words, God's assessment of "very good" could well be understood as God's concluding, "That's just what I wanted!" Creation, including us, the work of his hands, is just what the Creator wanted! God created us out of his desire for us. Just like Job, we, too, can conclude that our existence alone is proof positive of the Creator's confession of love for us.

Third-Party Observers

Is God's love observable by others? Is the love of God something that can be seen and appreciated by others just like the love shared between friends, spouses, or parents and children? Some writers of the Bible think the answer is yes. One writer concluded, "the earth is full of the steadfast love of the LORD" (Psalm 33:5). In his mind, there is plenty of evidence for God's love all around us. We just need to be willing to see it. In fact, so important was this observation that an affirmation of God's love became a central component of one of the very few, but often repeated, creeds found in the pages of the Old Testament: "The steadfast love of the LORD never ceases, his mercies never come to an end" (Lamentations 3:22).

The proclamation that the love of God never ceases became embedded in an often used chorus from ancient Israel (2 Chronicles 5:13; 7:3, 6; Ezra 3:11) and resides at the heart of several psalms (118:1–4, 29; and particularly Psalm 136).

Several places in the Bible indicate that the love of God is observable and leaves its mark upon its intended recipient. Evidence of God's love is observable by the way it amplifies and reproduces itself in the life of the recipient, both negatively (Luke 11:42) and positively (1 John 2:5; 5:3). One writer was convinced that the love given by

God expressed itself in both the sacrifice of the Son and the resultant quality of life experienced by those benefiting from the Son's gift. The love of the Creator is magnified and reproduced in the love now given by those loved!

> Beloved, let us love one another, because love is from God; everyone who loves is born of God and knows God. Whoever does not love does not know God, for God is love. *God's love was revealed among us in this way: God sent his only Son into the world so that we might live through him.* In this is love, not that we loved God but that he loved us and sent his Son to be the atoning sacrifice for our sins. Beloved, since God loved us so much, we also ought to love one another. No one has ever seen God; if we love one another, God lives in us, and his love is perfected in us. By this we know that we abide in him and he in us, because he has given us of his Spirit. (1 John 4:7–13 NRSV, emphasis added)

The writer of the gospel of John shared the conviction that the love of God is evidenced, plainly seen by all around, in the way that it affects its recipients: "I in them and thou in me, that they may become perfectly one, so that the world may know that thou hast sent me and hast loved them even as thou hast loved me" (John 17:23).

If I want to find evidence that God is Lover, I should look for traces of that love in the people around me. Those who have been touched by God's love are changed. That change is beyond our own ability to produce and not simply a result of growing wiser and maturing with age. This change comes from outside our horizon and outside our control and has the potential to affect generations to come. The psalmist wrote, "The steadfast love of the LORD is from everlasting to everlasting on those who fear him, and his righteousness to children's children" (Psalm 103:17 NRSV).

Clearly, when we take time to think about it, we see ample reason to conclude that God does love us—each one. The evidence is all around.

BETWIXT AND BETWEEN

As we bring our discussion of God the Creator, Redeemer, and Lover to a conclusion, perhaps it's time to reassemble the pieces. Even though we focused on separate aspects of God in the previous three chapters, we must now recognize that in reality, God, like any other person, can never be dissected in this fashion. Creation, redemption, and love are inseparably intertwined in the person we call God. Creation and redemption are equally and fully acts of love. Redemption is creative and creation is redemptive.

If you are like me, the previous paragraph elicits a deep-felt tension. I don't always feel, nor can I always experience, the breadth and depth of love in creation or redemption. I get glimpses now and then of the potential and possibilities of love's redemptive and creative designs, but all too quickly those glimpses are overwhelmed by the press of a reality in need of redemption.

I'm not the only one to feel this way. In fact, a famous passage from the New Testament expresses the same tension. Notice the writer's complaint is that the best and even special sources of knowledge available (tongues, knowledge, prophecy) are insufficient to provide a clear picture of the creative and redemptive reality love has in store. The glimpses of that reality we occasionally are afforded produce a longing for more.

> Love never ends. But as for prophecies, they will come to an end; as for tongues, they will cease; as for knowledge, it will come to an end. For we know only in part, and we prophesy only in part; but when the complete comes, the partial will come to an end. When I was a child, I spoke like a child, I thought like a child, I reasoned like a child; when I became an adult, I put an

end to childish ways. For now we see in a
mirror, dimly, but then we will see face to
face. Now I know only in part; then I will
know fully, even as I have been fully known.
And now faith, hope, and love abide, these
three; and the greatest of these is love.
(1 Corinthians 13:8–13 NRSV)

For a great many of us it is easy to be overwhelmed
by the nagging suspicion that it's all too good to be true.
Having been beaten down and disappointed, many among
us become afraid to hope, afraid to dream, and afraid
to believe that a future is in store. It's to us that Jesus
directed his words. Sometimes in a quiet whisper but often
in unbounded joy he shouts his offer:

Come to me, all you that are weary and are
carrying heavy burdens, and I will give you
rest. Take my yoke upon you, and learn from
me; for I am gentle and humble in heart, and
you will find rest for your souls. For my yoke
is easy, and my burden is light. (Matthew
11:28–30 NRSV)

Until that time, I long for more. Like all-too-infrequent
visits with a best friend now living miles away, my glimpses
of the redeemed reality formed by the Creator's love tide

me over and add to my trust that more is on the way. Faith, hope, and love become a way of life while I wait for the completion of the Creator's redemptive love.

WHERE TO BE FOUND?

Before we leave this chapter, I'm forced to return to a question that has been haunting me for some time. Earlier in this chapter, we looked at the effect the love of the Creator has on those loved. At least according to the testimony of the biblical writers, the Creator's love is evidenced in the way it is magnified and reproduced in the lives of those living in conscious awareness of that love. When I wrote those words I became plagued by a lingering question I now feel we must consider explicitly. That question is simply: Where?

Where do I see this kind of love in people? When I honestly attempt to be aware of the magnified and reproduced love of God expressing itself in the lives of people, where do I see it most frequently? As near as I can tell, I see this love of the Creator reflected in people who are most willing to reach out and value others despite personal differences. I see this love among those who have a glimpse of the breadth of redemption and find joy in the things and people around them. I see the love of God among those who see all of creation susceptible to God's redeeming love. I see it among those who mourn with others, even half a world away, suffering from the horrible results of war or natural catastrophe. I see it in people who live mindful that all humanity is precious. I see it in people attempting to construct lives that value people more than things.

But here's my problem: I do not see this love of God any more present among religious people than among nonreligious people. In fact, my observations lead me to suspect that religious people have their own special set of obstacles hindering the magnification and replication of God's love through them. In my experience at least, the reflected love of God is often only poorly seen in committed religious adherents whose driving intent is on remaking others into their own religious image. I see the reflected love of God least in those who would hoard the grace of God and act as if they were its only custodians, gatekeepers to whom everyone else must turn. I see the love of God least in those who would vainly turn that love into a commodity by which to purchase their own prestige. I see the love of God least in those who make it part of their business plan to reach financial success. I'm ashamed to say, I see the love of God least among theologians and religious professionals competing to produce the best program or brand by which the love of God would be known.

The most uncomfortable part of my observation is that by no means do I exclude myself from the critique. I, too, struggle with my own personal hesitancy to let God's love become my preferred way of life; and I struggle mightily with religious claims, rituals, and customs that compete for ownership of that love. I understand all too well the feeling captured by Paul when he wrote, "For I do not do the good I want, but the evil I do not want is what I do" (Romans 7:19).

Paul and I are not the only members of this self-torn group. There are many of us who see a growing disconnect between religious observance and time spent with God. Yet, I know full well and am convinced that for most people, pursuit of God takes on a religious hue. For many, the tensions enveloping this dilemma have proven too much, and a great number have dropped out of any meaningful quest to know God.

But rather than simply using the failure of this or that religious institution as a convenient escape from the demands of a sincere search for God, let's turn our attention elsewhere. What would it look like to spend time with God? No matter where they're found, religious or not, what qualities characterize those who truly experience intimacy with God? These questions will lead us to the next part of our journey together.

Part 4
The Company You Keep

As kids we were advised to pick our friends carefully. We were told, "You become like the company you keep." The same—and more—is true with the God you choose. All of us will inevitably imitate what we worship. So the question is: Which characteristics of God become part and parcel of those who seek to look through the hole in the sky?

7
Talk to Me

As a Child

As a child, I learned the proper way to talk with God. It involved closing my eyes (if I peeked it certainly wouldn't work) and folding my hands. Without knowing it, I think I often endeavored to enter into a trancelike state of meditation, devoid of external stimuli (therefore the closed eyes and hands-off posture) when I prayed. I soon learned that certain words and particular inflections or ways of saying those words often helped me sound more spiritual and so more likely to impress God. At least that's what I thought when I heard other people intoning those words and using those inflections. A special prayer language, spoken with fervor and intensity, was sure to catch God's attention. And if this prayer was attended to by others with the occasional "amen," "Yes, Lord," or pious-sounding sigh and "ummm," then for sure God would be impressed with what was being said and all sorts of divine boons would be granted.

Only alone and at night before drifting off to sleep would my special prayer language disappear as I was reduced to desperate pleas for divine assistance concerning the more practical aspects of my ten-year-old world. Miraculous help to do well on an impending math or history exam, for which I did not prepare, escape from the class bully, or, best of all, a snow day canceling school were frequent topics of my conversations with God when we were all alone. I certainly couldn't pray for something as selfish as a grade on a test amid sighs, ummms, and yes-Lords! But hiding under the covers on a cold winter night with not a single "thee," "bestow," or "givest" to be heard and with eyes wide open, it was hard to think that the Divine was giving me much consideration.

Years have passed since those late-night conversations with God. But thinking back on those times, I must now confess it is most likely that those were the conversations to which God listened most intently. For it was right then, while hiding under the covers, that I spoke most honestly with my Creator, Redeemer, and Lover.

BUT NOW

Since those late-night conversations, I've learned a lot (and had to unlearn even more!) about God. One of my most cherished lessons, and one I need to review from time to time, takes me back to something I think many of us know intuitively as children but tend to forget as we get older: God values honesty. In prayer, this means God wants us to simply tell him what's on our minds, no matter how unspiritual, trivial, or mundane it might be. Our getting to know God will involve quality time spent with the Divine, and that quality time will inevitably include conversation. Therefore, it seems worthwhile to think together about prayer as we pursue our quest to find a hole in the sky.

PROSE PRAYER IN THE OLD TESTAMENT

I would like to direct our search first to a series of incidents written about in the pages of the Bible. Scattered throughout the Old Testament are a number of episodes in which people pray to God as part of an unfolding narrative and story in which those people are playing a part.[47] The

---

47   Passages where these prayers are mentioned: Genesis 20:7, 12; 25:21; 30:6, 22; 47:31; Exodus 2:23–24; 9:29, 33; 14:10, 15; 22:22; Leviticus 9:24; 16:21; 26:40; Numbers 11:2; 21:7; Deuteronomy 9:20; Judges 3:9; 1 Samuel 1:10, 12–15; 7:5, 8–9; 8:6, 18; 12:17–19, 23; 15:11; 2 Samuel 6:18; 12:16; 21:1; 1 Kings 13:6; 18:42; 2 Kings 4:33; Isaiah 42:2–4; 56:7; Jeremiah 21:2; Ezekiel 22:30; Lamentations 3:8, 44; Daniel 2:18; 6:11; Ezra 8:21–23; Nehemiah 2:4; 4:3; 1 Chronicles 5:20; 21:26; 2 Chronicles 33:12–13. Passages in which the words of prayer occur: Genesis 17:18; 18:23–32; 19:18–19; 24:11, 26–27; 28:3–4; 29:35; 30:24; 32:10–13; 43:14; 48:15–16; Exodus 4:13; 5:22–23; 17:4; 18:9; 32:11–13; 32:31–32; Numbers 11:11–15; 12:13; 14:13–19; 16:15, 22; 22:34; 27:16–17; Deuteronomy 1:11; 3:23–25; 9:25–29; Joshua 7:6–9; 7:25; 10:12; Judges 5:24; 6:36–37, 39; 1:10, 15; 13:8; 15:18; 16:23–24; 16:28; 21:2–3; 1 Samuel 7:6; 12:10; 25:32; 2 Samuel 3:29, 39; 7:18–29; 12:13; 14:17; 15:31; 18:28; 24:3, 10, 17; 1 Kings 1:36, 47; 3:6–9; 8:15–21, 22–23, 47, 55–61; 10:9; 17:20–21; 18:36–37; 19:4; 2 Kings 6:17–18, 20; 19:15–19; 20:2–3; Jeremiah 3:22–25; 4:10; 7:16; (11:14; 14:11); 14:7–9, 19–22; 15:15–18; 16:19; 17:14–18; 18:19–23; 20:7–13; Ezekiel 9:8; Amos 7:2, 7; Jonah 1:14; 9:2; Ruth 1:8–9; 2:4, 12; 4:11, 14; Daniel 2:19–23; 9:4–19; Ezra 9:6–15; Nehemiah 1:4–11; 3:36; 5:19 (6:14; 13:14, 22, 29, 31); 1 Chronicles 4:10; 29:10–19; 2 Chronicles 13:14–15; 14:10; 20:5–12; 30:18–19.

stories of these different people and their prayers are told to us as teachable moments from which we, as observers, can learn something about how these people related with God. The prayers have a great deal to teach us and some of them are presented as models from which we can learn.

What is common to all these prayers, coming from the drama of real life, is that they are simple and direct. There is no special prayer language used to form a petition to God, and there is a tremendous amount of freedom in these cries to God. In fact, if the address prefacing the prayer didn't give it away, or if by reading the story in which the prayer is found you didn't already know, there is little in the actual wording of the prayer to let you know it is God being addressed. The prayers take their cue from the normal everyday kind of conversation we use with each other. The prayers are expressed in a profound simplicity and directness. They contain no hint of incantation or magical formula by which to attract the divine attention. Absent magical words that, when breathed, force a divine response, what is it that gives to these prayers their effectiveness? It must be simply this: God values honesty. As with human-to-human conversation, when we address God in prayer, the effectiveness of our words depends on the degree to which those words are authentically expressed, believable, and sincere. "Have I got a deal for you!" when spoken by a trusted friend has a totally different effect than if those same words come to us from a used car dealer with a reputation for passing off lemons to any unwary buyer. The same is with God. The character of the one speaking to God determines the believability of what is spoken. This is truly amazing! God wants us to be real and authentic when we are in conversation with him. No amount of pious language or accompanying ritual and pomp can ever replace the value given to simple honesty and authenticity when we pray. The honesty and authenticity demanded by God in prayer works itself out in three important ideas that are worthy of our attention as we strive to know God. These three ideas can be framed into one sentence we will unpack and examine more thoroughly: *Anyone, anytime, anywhere can pray with head held high, for God is ever near.*

Anyone, Anytime, Anywhere

The ability to approach God in prayer, absent form or ritual, means that prayer is not conditioned by time, place, or even person. In the Old Testament, an Israelite or a non-Israelite alike may speak to God in prayer. The person in prayer might be in an Israelite religious place or in a non-Israelite temple. The person praying might be in a cave, a home, working the fields, waking in the morning, preparing for sleep at night. The place doesn't matter, for the cry of the distressed reaches God regardless of who is praying—anywhere, anytime. Every human being is capable of speaking with God according to his or her own specific need. We need only be sincere. The value of sincerity when talking to God is reinforced throughout the Old Testament (1 Samuel 1:15; 7:3; Psalms 145:18; 78:34–37; Job 11:13; Isaiah 29:13; Hosea 7:14). Since prayer is built upon sincerity and not some special ritual or verbal formula, everyone can freely resort to prayer! Anyone so moved by gratitude, admiration, or need and desperation is free to approach the Divine in prayer. This means that prayer can be a frequent occurrence and need not be regulated to special places at special times. Not only can famous and important people like Rachel or Leah pray, but any woman can, with equal hope, pour out her heart to God. Not only could a king like David, but any father can pray for a sick infant (1 Kings 3:38). Anyone, anywhere, anytime—in prayer, God is available to us all.

When inhibition is overcome by great need or great love, prayer is given voice.

With Head Held High

This immediately accessible means of communicating with God has a spinoff effect for those engaged in prayer with God. There is a remarkable equality resident in prayer. Prophet, priest, or king—all are treated alike with the most common and ordinary. With no need to seek out the mediation of a priest or other high-ranking person, our access to God in prayer means we are all equally important to the Divine.

Our access to God in prayer should impress upon all of us how important we are to God. And just as those who have access to the most powerful and important are expected to act accordingly, so, too, our privileged access to God implies a responsibility given to us all. The open invitation extended to us in prayer means that all of us are to hold our heads high and behave in a manner befitting those with access to Deity. The Old Testament talks about this privilege in terms of creating a holy nation and a nation of priests (Exodus 19:6). The same is alluded to in the New Testament and applied to those who, despite all outward appearances to the contrary, are accorded special status simply because they have approached near to God (1 Peter 2:5–6).

Only those with a special invitation may approach the Lord of all. You and I are recipients of that special invitation.

> Since, then, we have a great high priest who has passed through the heavens, Jesus, the Son of God, let us hold fast to our confession. For we do not have a high priest who is unable to sympathize with our weaknesses, but we have one who in every respect has been tested as we are, yet without sin. Let us therefore approach the throne of grace with

boldness, so that we may receive mercy and find grace to help in time of need. (Hebrews 4:14–16 NRSV)

For God Is Ever Near

The question made famous by a wireless phone company—"Can you hear me now?"—is always met with a divine "Yes," for God is never out of range and never considers adding a roaming charge to those who seek him in prayer. The ever-present means of communicating with God by prayer has a second consequence, in addition to creating a remarkable sense of egalitarian dignity.

Even as frequent conversation allows us to keep our friends and family members foremost in mind, so, too, frequent conversation with God allows us to maintain a permanent link to the Divine. For those whose stories we read about in the pages of the Old Testament, this line of communication, constantly open and instantly available, reinforced the vivid reality of God's presence in even the most mundane and everyday aspects of life. The same is available to us.

But unlike the technology of mobile phones, prayer relies on no technological wonders to bring the speakers together—or to separate them. While walking around a college campus I have seen some strange things. What follows still causes me to scratch my head. Not so long ago, on a bright and crisp fall afternoon, I found myself walking behind a student engrossed in a conversation on her cell phone. As we walked, the person with whom she was talking fell in step right next to her. They smiled at each other, fully acknowledging each other's presence, but continued the conversation on the phone, even though they were standing only inches apart. For these two people, their cell phones provided only the semblance of personal interaction as the technology of the cell phone, intended to bring them together, actually separated them. Prayer is different. Both as honest expression to God and as patient listening to a voice from God, prayer has no such barriers.

TEACH US TO PRAY

The New Testament builds upon these remarkable ideas about prayer found in the Old Testament and adds a few ideas of its own. On one occasion, Jesus was asked directly by several of his disciples for help in improving the way they accessed God in prayer (Luke 11:1–4). What I find interesting about the way the question is framed in Luke 11 is that the request was posed after they observed Jesus pray. In Luke 11, the disciples saw something very attractive about the way Jesus was able to communicate with God and they wanted in on it, so they simply asked Jesus: "Lord, teach us to pray, as John taught his disciples" (Luke 11:1). The last half of their request ("as John taught his disciples") implies that prayer was recognized as a means of gaining status, certainly with other people and perhaps with God, too. Both Jesus and John were recognized as people of importance, and Jesus' disciples were convinced that if they could only pray like Jesus, then they too would be recognized, even by God, as individuals of importance. Prayer used as a means of climbing the social ladder seems to have been fairly common and is clearly behind the criticism leveled by Jesus in Matthew 6:5–6. For this reason the request in Luke 11 by Jesus' disciples has a double edge to it. They observed Jesus in prayer (verse 1) and concluded that he was pretty good at it— good enough that they wanted in on it, good enough that they wanted to be able to share in both the effectiveness of prayer and the status that effectiveness would bring.

Jesus' reply is both amazing and exhilarating! I suspect that in reply to the disciples' request Jesus could have said, "Sorry, but you folks will never make it. You see, I have a special in, and God won't listen to you in the way he listens to me. I'm way more important than you. After all, I *am* the Son of God, and the Father pays much closer attention when *I* speak."

But nothing like this is said. Instead, Jesus launches into a simple and direct prayer pattern followed by several analogies designed to make very plain that God is just as concerned about their prayers as he is about Jesus' own prayers! The prayer begins: "Father..." This one word takes

away all concern for social positioning. For the one praying, there is no more status to achieve, no more ladders
to climb. The one praying already has the right to call God
"Father." When we stop to consider the full impact of this
one opening word, the prayer Jesus taught becomes even
more astounding!

The simple pattern of prayer must have made quite an
impact, for Matthew uses it too (a slightly expanded version), placing it right smack in the middle of the Sermon
on the Mount in Matthew 6:8–13. The model provided by
Jesus reinforces much of what we've already discovered
about prayer from the Old Testament.

> Do not be like them, for your Father knows
> what you need before you ask him. Pray then
> in this way: Our Father in heaven, hallowed
> be your name. Your kingdom come. Your will
> be done, on earth as it is in heaven. Give us
> this day our daily bread. And forgive us our
> debts, as we also have forgiven our debt-
> ors. And do not bring us to the time of trial,
> but rescue us from the evil one. (Matthew
> 6:8–13 NRSV)

Both here in Matthew 6:9 and also in Luke 11:2 the
introduction to the prayer indicates that it was intended as
a model for prayer and not as a specific prayer formulation

to be used over and over. It wasn't given by Jesus as a formal or ritualistic way of speaking with God. In contrast to those who go on and on for show, Jesus admonishes the disciples: don't prattle, don't be concerned about using big words, and don't mouth repetitions that fail to unleash the intent of the heart. Sincerity, honesty, and simplicity seem to be the watchwords here. This simplicity is possible because "your Father knows what you need." The confidence of being heard is not contingent upon flowery language, proper posture, linguistic formula, or even social standing. In a manner quite in line with the prayers we saw in the Old Testament, the one praying can have confidence that she or he is being heard—simply because of our Father's character. Jesus gave to us a great gift when he taught us to pray.

ONLY FOR THE BRAVE

Even though this prayer (sometimes called the Lord's Prayer) is familiar to many, with some even learning it word for word as young children, seldom do we stop and consider the radical—even dangerous—nature of the prayer. At heart, the prayer is a prayer for an invasion. It is a request that the kingdom of heaven invade earth. It is a prayer that the norms and ethics, the way of behaving and the manner of life consistent with the kingdom of heaven be realized right here and right now. The prayer is nothing less than a plea for a worldwide revolution in which the kingdoms we know and by which we live become turned inside out and upside down—reorganized according to the norms of a kingdom not of this world. What makes the prayer dangerous is that *it is implicit in the prayer that the one praying consent to be a willing participant in this invasion.* The person giving expression to this prayer recognizes an absolute dependence upon the Father. That dependence includes reliance upon the Father for the necessities of daily life and for repeated forgiveness. Perhaps most of all, this dependence on the Father reaches to reliance upon God for escape from an all-too-frequent bent toward selfishness and the allure of the counter-invasion (everything at odds with a life in the kingdom of heaven). In other words, the one willing to pray for the arrival of the kingdom of heaven is positioned as the forward guard—the promise and evidence of more to come. This prayer is a serious matter, and if—as we have seen consistently throughout the Bible—God values honesty and sincerity in prayer, we should all think twice before speaking these words to God. The prayer taught by Jesus in Luke 11 and Matthew 6 is only for the brave—or only for those who have nothing else to lose.

Courage is offered in two ways throughout this short prayer. The prayer begins with a reminder of the holiness of God. "Hallowed be your name" is a phrase that recognizes and gives glory and honor to God. The name is simply another way of referring to the person. So, with this phrase the prayer begins with a reminder to treat God as God. The character of the Father gives confidence that the disciple's prayer is heard, and recognition of God's character gives guidance in knowing how to pray. What could possibly motivate a person to pray this prayer? Why would someone willingly let go of all this world has to offer in favor of a kingdom not yet seen? Simply this: because God is God.

Courage is also offered at the end of the prayer. The prayer ends with a request for forgiveness from sin.[48] The request for forgiveness is not a hopeless and vague wish for some impossibility (a wish to discover gold in the backyard). Nor is the request for forgiveness some perfunctory and routine but meaningless custom like the way we frequently greet each other by asking, "How are you?" without really wanting an answer. The request for forgiveness of sin in this prayer is an opportunity to reinforce the interpersonal relationship that is assumed throughout the prayer. The request for forgiveness carries with it recognition that the Creator, Redeemer, and Lover—sovereign over all the universe—is also and best known as Father. There is no false piety resident in these words, nor is there a debilitating guilt that clouds everything else. The request for forgiveness implies a realistic assessment of our own imperfectness.

---

48   Matthew's use of *debt* (6:13) is a different way of saying something very close to that meant by the use of the word *sin* found in Luke 11:4.

And the request for forgiveness is a celebration of the overwhelming and unstoppable redemption and love the Creator has toward the one praying. The celebration is assured, for it has been guaranteed by the Father, who knows what we need even before we ask.

The request for forgiveness is amplified by a reminder of the disciple's family likeness to the Father in 6:14–15. Having been forgiven, the disciple is capable of extending the same to others (Mark 11:25; Matthew 18:34–35). But there's more. Not only is the disciple capable of forgiving; the disciple is held accountable by the Father to forgive. It is incumbent upon the disciple—one who recognizes the character of God and is praying for the invasion of the kingdom of heaven—to act in concert with both.

There is a deep joy here. The disciple is forgiven by the Father, freed from a weight and stain that no amount of effort could remove. The emphasis here is not upon the despicable character of the disciple who stands in such great need of forgiveness. Rather, the emphasis is upon the fact of having been forgiven! So, freed from a great burden to earn a righteousness surpassing that of the scribes and Pharisees, the disciple can pray freely, live freely, and forgive freely. Forgiveness is a corrective lens that allows the disciple to see clearly—to see clearly herself or himself, to see clearly her or his relationship to the Father, and to see clearly other people (7:3–4). *Forgiven* becomes a fundamental characteristic of self-identification for the disciple. The disciple is forgiven. First and last, the disciple is forgiven.

THE GOD WHO IS NEAR

In many ways, I've discovered that my prayers are often appeals to the Divine for an experience of what God claims to be. In prayer, I ask the Creator to act toward me in the beneficial manners that are dictated by the divine character. I want God to be near to me and I want God to be near to those for whom I pray. But sometimes that nearness is not at all evident and, often my appeals in prayer are motivated by a devastating loss of that sense of nearness. It is because I can't sense the Creator's nearness, because I can't see the evidence of God's character that I ask for divine nearness. Many people have prayed in this way, and a good number of the prayers in the book of Psalms are motivated the same way. Psalm 34:18 (NRSV) is a good example: "The LORD is near to the brokenhearted, and saves the crushed in spirit."

The prayer is laden with contradictions, and these contradictions get right to the heart of the prayer. The cause for prayer is the apparent absence of God, but the very act of prayer supposes that God is near to answer. If the Lord is near, there is no reason to be brokenhearted or crushed in spirit. But if God is distant, there is no reason to pray. If God is distant, he is not even within divine earshot—or at least not close enough to prevent, or at the very least empathize with, the heartache. It is this disappointment, confusion, and contradiction that give voice to the desperate cry in prayer.

This particular prayer (Psalm 34) aggravates the consternation, for it presupposes that the brokenhearted and crushed in spirit of the verse we already quoted are righteous (verses 15, 17). The Lord hears them, sees clearly their plight, and is quick to deliver them from their predicament. The wicked, however, receive no such assurance (verse 16). In fact, the Lord is against them and is quite happy if no one remembers them (verse 16). Evil people deserve what they get, and the Lord is not near to assist them. While the righteous may also suffer affliction, "the LORD delivers him out of them all" (verse 19).

But this isn't how life works, at least as far as I—or this psalmist—can see. There are very good people who have gotten the short end of life's stick and some very bad people who seem to be doing just fine. Likewise, it isn't always obvious and clear to all that God is alert and attending to the needs of the righteous. The writer of a psalm just a few pages later may have never seen "the righteous forsaken or [their] children begging bread" (Psalm 37:25), but I have, sometimes horribly so. God's apparent absence, with the resultant dissolution of all the normal rules for right and wrong, forms the dilemma of prayer here in Psalm 34 and in many of my own prayers. This dilemma is felt in another psalm: "Draw near to me, redeem me, set me free because of my enemies" (Psalm 69:18 NRSV).

This psalm is an anguished cry from a heart experiencing unrelenting tragedy. Since December 26, 2004, the beginning of this psalm has had special significance to me. Verse 1 reads, "Save me, O God! For the waters have come up to my neck."

The Indian Ocean tsunami permitted no meaningful discrimination between the righteous and the wicked. It gave no time but for the briefest and most desperate cry for help: "Save me, O God!" This alone is the essence of our pleas to God in prayer. Voiced in desperation and absolute need, the cry is an honest and sincere plea for God to be near. Oddly, the prayer is both the vehicle of request and the reassurance of divine response.

As a Child

We will end this chapter where we began—in childhood. My journey of learning and relearning about conversation with God has taken me back to those nights under the covers when, with eyes wide open and using only the simplest of words, I told God what was on my mind. Children tend to be authentic and sincere, transparent and pure, in their conversations. I'm learning, much too late, that, as with any mother, this is exactly what God cherishes when her children speak with her (Hosea 11:3–4). It's this kind of conversation that the divine Father loves to hear (Mark 10:14–15).

But now it's time to ask those three questions designed to help us test our provisionally accepted knowledge of God: Is it reliable? Does it make sense? Does it work?

Anyone, anytime, anywhere, can pray with head held high, for God is ever near. This is the core statement that has guided us in this chapter. When placed within the majestic sweep of the biblical portrayal, the first two parts of our fundamental premise—(1) anyone, anywhere, anytime and (2) with head held high—find no problem passing the tests of authority and coherence. Both seem reasonable if indeed the Creator is also the Redeemer and Lover. The difficulty comes with the addition of the third part of our premise—for God is ever near—and the application of the third test: Does it work? Is God actually near me when I pray? The majestic sweep of the biblical portrayal describes a created universe susceptible to the intrusive presence of God, but is there experiential evidence to confirm that God is near, and what kind of evidence would be sufficient to make a determination?

If we look only for a positive reply to requests made in prayer as evidence for God's nearness, then the conclusion is inescapable: God is, at best, unreliably near. But common sense and experience argue against this simple test for God's presence. Only spoiled children who cannot tolerate being denied blame that denial upon the carelessness and neglect of the one being petitioned. No, there must be more. An immediate and agreeable response to our petitions cannot be the only sign of God's presence.

Perhaps we can begin looking for an answer to the question Does it work? by considering another question: What would God's absence look like? Why does the absence of God create disappointment if God is typically absent? Wouldn't we have gotten used to God's aloofness by now? Perhaps our persistent anxiety resulting from the feeling of divine abandonment is because we were made for something different. It isn't our natural state, and just like deprivation of food, water, or the air we breathe leads to noticeable discomfort, so, too, does a sense of God's absence. Our discomfort is heightened in prayer, for all too often we articulate requests in prayer only out of great need and urgency. Any delay is intolerable. It's intolerable because we were made for something different.

SO HOW DO I BEGIN?

If you are ready to try prayer and see if there is any experience of the Deity to be had, how to begin? As we've seen from our survey of the biblical models, a good place to begin is with simple honesty and sincerity. Prayer may be one of the best opportunities for you to really be you. Remember, the Creator fashioned you just the way you are with all your peculiar idiosyncrasies and quirks, so there is nothing to be uncomfortable about. I seriously doubt that you could tell God anything to shock him or rob you of her love. One person told me, "When I pray, I have the opportunity to tell Someone things that I could rarely imagine telling anyone else." This isn't a bad place to begin. But let me add one little bit more. When you pray, don't forget to listen for a reply. I suspect it won't be in an audible voice, and perhaps it won't come right away. For me, God is best heard in a quiet and still place. Maybe it will be the same for you.

8

Put Your Money Where Your Mouth Is Or You Are What You Spend

"You are what you eat." We've all heard this as a dietary warning to be mindful of what (and how much) we are becoming. Despite the popularity of the truism, I suspect Jesus might quibble with its validity. If Mathew 15:11 is accurate, Jesus was of the opinion that it's not what you put into your mouth that defines you, but it's what comes out of your mouth that reveals your character. And if we grant that the Bible is somehow or other associated with the "word of God," then those things appearing most prominently in the Bible reveal to us something about the character of God. Just like us, what comes out of God's "mouth" reveals something about the Deity's character as well. Far and away, one of the most recurrent themes in the Bible is treatment of the poor. This recurring theme reveals to us something of the character of God. God cares for the poor. If we are to progress in our journey to discover a hole in the sky, we must explore God's care for the poor, for, as we will soon learn, he expects those who would know him to mimic his care.

OLD TESTAMENT

There are a number of words used in the Old Testament to describe the poor. Although each word has a slightly different meaning and nuance, there is a fair amount of overlap among them and each is best understood within the context of the specific passage in which it is used. In the broad aggregate, in the pages of the Old Testament, the poor are those who are forced to go without. They lack the economic or political and legal resources to be able to make their own way in the world. The poor are the powerless.

Protection for the Powerless

Some of the legal texts in the Old Testament make very plain that the poor are to be cared for, even if it requires the redistribution of food and other necessities, taking the excess from those who have an abundance (Exodus 23:10–11; Isaiah 32:6–7; Ezekiel 16:49; Psalm 132:15). The poor are not to be discriminated against in court (Exodus 23:3, 6; Leviticus 19:15) or on the job (Deuteronomy 24:14-15). The legal texts and prophetic texts consider the community's treatment of the poor a matter of utmost importance, and this priority is reflected in the reform description found in Nehemiah 5:1–13.

Some of the prophets demonstrate amazing deference to the poor. The economically and socially advantaged, those who might be tempted to use their power in the acquisition of even more power and privilege at the expense of the poor, are given harsh warnings (Isaiah 10:2; 11:4; 14:30; 26:6; Amos 2:7; 4:1; 5:11). In Isaiah, God holds the poor in special regard and will not delegate their care to someone else. God places himself at their disposal.

> For thou hast been a stronghold to the poor,
> A stronghold to the needy in his distress,
> A shelter from the storm and a shade from
> the heat. (Isaiah 25:4)

God is the hope for the poor (Isaiah 11:4; 29:19; 61:1), for he is their rescue (Habakkuk 3:13–14; Zephaniah 3:12).

Social Responsibility

Just like many today, the writers in the book of Proverbs struggled to find a balance when considering the plight of the poor. On one hand, we find admonitions that are quick to emphasize the personal responsibility the poor have to better their own lot, while, at the same time, writers in

Proverbs highlight the communal responsibility to care for the poor.

The idea of personal responsibility is plain in the very clear warnings to those predisposed toward laziness by predicting poverty as the outcome of their irresponsible behavior (Proverbs 6:10–11; 21:5; 24:33–34; 28:19). Likewise, get-rich-quick schemes, shortcuts, and extravagance are to be avoided, for these, too, lead to impoverished ends (Proverbs 14:23; 21:17; 28:22). On the other hand, the poor are not to be neglected or abused by the community. There are clear warnings against those who might be tempted to see the poor as easy targets for profit taking (Proverbs 21:13; 22:16, 22; 28:3, 8, 15). Instead, those who act kindly toward the poor demonstrate wisdom and righteousness (Proverbs 22:9; 28:27; 29:7; 31:9, 20). In fact, any act of kindness extended toward the poor is considered an act of kindness done to God himself.

> He who oppresses a poor man insults his Maker, but he who is kind to the needy honors him. (Proverbs 14:31)
> He who is kind to the poor lends to the Lord, and he will repay him for his deed. (Proverbs 19:17; and perhaps echoed in Matthew 25:31–36)

Likewise, warnings against taking advantage of the poor are well heeded.

> Do not remove an ancient landmark or enter
> the fields of the fatherless;
> for their Redeemer is strong; he will plead
> their cause against you. (Proverbs 23:10–11)

The book of Job shares many of the sentiments found in Proverbs. Job's own misfortune and poverty is interpreted by his friends as the result of some great sin or lack of piety. Prominent among the accusations against which Job must defend himself is that he has mistreated the poor (20:10, 19). In reply, Job mounts his defense against this allegation by citing instances of his own kindness to the poor (29:16; 30:25; 31:16). The strength of Job's defense depends upon the underlying premise that, in his kindness toward the poor, Job has mimicked the behavior of God himself.

> But he [God] saves the fatherless from their
> [the unscrupulous rich] mouth,
> The needy from the hand of the mighty.
> So the poor have hope, and injustice shuts
> her mouth. (Job 5:15–16)

God Cares for the Poor

It's in the psalms that we see most clearly the character of God expressed in his care for the poor. Because God is known to have compassion on the weak and the needy (Psalm 72:13), prayers can be made to enlist his defense and deliverance (Psalm 72:4). Reminiscent of Job 5:15–16, Psalm 82:3–4 also recognizes that God holds in special regard the weak, fatherless, afflicted, and needy (Psalm 113:7). God will not forget the poor (Psalm 9:18; 10:14; 12:5; 18:27; 22:24; 34:6; 35:10; 40:17; 68:10; 69:33; 70:5; 140:12; 147:6; 149:4), and those who would partner with God in his care for the poor are themselves highly regarded.

> Blessed is he who considers the poor!
> The LORD delivers him in the day of trouble;
> the LORD protects him and keeps him alive;
> he is called blessed in the land. (Psalm 41:1–2)

Perhaps God's compassion is summed up in the following selection from Psalm 72, in which a whole constellation of terms describing the poor is found packed tightly together.

> For he delivers the needy when he calls,
> the poor and him who has no helper.

He has pity on the weak and the needy,
and saves the lives of the needy.
From oppression and violence he redeems
their life;
and precious is their blood in his sight.
(Psalm 72:12–14)

In this psalm, God is portrayed as the last and best line of defense for those who have no place else to turn.

It could be said that Isaiah speaks for all the Hebrew prophets when he admonishes the would-be "people of God" to

cease to do evil,
learn to do good;
seek justice,
correct oppression;
defend the fatherless,
plead for the widow. (Isaiah 1:16–17)

Or, consider the words of Amos addressed to those who "buy the poor for silver and the needy for a pair of sandals" (8:6): "Let justice roll down like waters, and righteousness like an ever-flowing stream" (5:24); and Micah, who graphically described the abusers of the powerless as those "who tear the skin from off my people, and their flesh from off their bones" (Micah 3:2).

What should these atrocious offenders do to remedy their misdeeds?

> He has showed you, O man, what is good;
> and what does the LORD require of you but
> to do justice, and to love kindness, and to
> walk humbly with your God? (Micah 6:8)

The poor, captives, blind, and oppressed are the foremost objects of the Creator's redeeming love.

NEW TESTAMENT

As in the Old Testament, there are a number of words used by New Testament authors to describe the plight and condition of the poor. And like its Old Testament predecessor, the New Testament paints a portrait of the poor as those who must go without the basic necessities required to sustain life. The poor are described variously as those in need of food, shelter, employment, security, dignity, clothing, and health.

To Preach Good News to the Poor

Significantly, the message of Jesus and thereby the thrust of the New Testament writers is to proclaim good news to the poor. Right from the beginning Luke presents

Jesus as all about caring for the poor. In fact, the very first public appearance of Jesus, mentioned by Luke, sets the direction for the rest of the book. While in a synagogue, Jesus stands to read, turns to Isaiah, and reads these words: "The Spirit of the Lord is upon me, because he has anointed me to preach good news to the poor" (Luke 4:18 quoting Isaiah 61:1–2).

Matthew, too, recognizes the centrality of caring for the poor in Jesus' list of priorities. The Sermon on the Mount, a concise and hard-hitting compilation of Jesus' teaching, addresses the poor in the opening line: "Blessed are the poor in spirit, for theirs is the kingdom of heaven" (Matthew 5:3).

Some have interpreted these words in Matthew to mean an attitude of dependency upon God rather than a literal focus on those in poverty. Luke, however, removes all doubt and reframes this opening line to read simply, "Blessed are you poor, for yours is the kingdom of God" (Luke 6:20).

This opening line from the sermon deserves a little more of our attention, for it truly is a remarkable statement. It doesn't promise some future great good but indicates that the poor have something now: the kingdom of God. The poor are to be congratulated (blessed), for they are the object of God's attention and have made their way into the kingdom of God! Either this is one of the cruelest statements of religious hoax ever uttered—an attempt to keep the poor from objecting to their plight—or Jesus could see into a reality that is hidden from the view of most other people. If there is truth to the statement that the poor are to be congratulated, then we must conclude it is simply because they are the object of God's care expressed in full and open membership to his kingdom and recipients of all the benefits that membership brings now and in the future.

Joining the Quest

The priority given to the poor and those in need, seen in this opening line from the Sermon on the Mount, is reinforced later in Matthew 11:2–6 (also Luke 7:18–23). Having heard rumors of the excitement Jesus was generating, John sent several of his disciples to Jesus to enquire about his authenticity. They wanted to know if Jesus was the Messiah, and so they asked very directly about his identity and credentials: "Are you he who is to come, or shall we look for another?" (Matthew 11:3).

In reply, Jesus cited evidence that was sufficient to remove all doubt, evidence that proved his involvement in the core priorities of the kingdom of God (as described in Isaiah 29:18–19):

> Go and tell John what you hear and see: the
> blind receive their sight and the lame walk,
> lepers are cleansed and the deaf hear, and

the dead are raised up, and the poor have
the good news preached to them. (Matthew
11:4–5)

And then for good measure, Jesus added, "And blessed
is he who takes no offense at me" (Matthew 11:6). In other
words, Jesus extended an invitation to others, welcom-
ing us to come and join his quest by adopting the same
priorities and behaviors—inviting us to participate in the
kingdom of God. Relief and rescue, freely giving to those
in need, are characteristics of the reign of God, for they
are characteristics of God.

One of the most radical statements on poverty found
in all the New Testament is Matthew 25:31–46. Perhaps
echoing the sentiment of Proverbs 19:17 and certainly
consistent with the divine identification in the company of
the poor found throughout the psalms, Matthew predicts a
future judgment of all humanity based solely on treatment
rendered toward the poor, marginalized, imprisoned, hun-
gry, and destitute. Acts of kindness committed toward these
unfortunates are considered acts of kindness extended
toward the King, and those turning a blind eye to the plight
of the poor do so at their own peril.

James, who among the New Testament writers stands
most immersed in the stream of the Old Testament prophets, envisions the embodiment of this good news preached
by Jesus in a community where rich and poor are treated

alike (1:9–11; 2:1–7) and among whom the law of love trumps the law of economics (1:8). Those who have gained wealth by taking advantage of the poor and defenseless are not to be envied, for their selfish behavior seals their condemnation (5:1–6).

Similar consideration for the poor, socially despised, and helpless can be found in Luke (1:51–53; 9:58; 12:32–34; 14:13). That concern is echoed in the strong corrective offered in 1 Corinthians 11 to those who would offer prestige within the believing community based upon wealth and power. Perhaps the most eloquent among all the New Testament writers to consider God's care for the poor is the writer of Hebrews. Throughout the book of Hebrews, the exodus of Hebrew slaves—the poorest of the poor—serves as the paradigm by which to understand God's redemptive work among humanity. The great list of heroes of the faith in chapter 11 climaxes with a litany of oppression and abuse, a description of the powerless who chose a kingdom not measured in silver and gold. The example provided by the heroes from the past is encouraged upon others, those choosing to be followers of Jesus and willingly entering the community of faith (10:32ff.). While waiting patiently for the appearance of a "kingdom that cannot be shaken" (12:28), the writer of Hebrews encourages us to

> Let brotherly love continue. Do not neglect to
> show hospitality to strangers.... Remember

those who are in prison … and those who are ill treated…. Let marriage be held in honor … and … Keep your life free from love of money. (Hebrews 13:1–5)

So What?

The consistent witness from the Bible is that God favors the poor. When we think about it, this divine preference for the poor only makes sense. If God is the Creator, Redeemer, and Lover, then it makes sense that those characteristics manifest themselves in action particularly toward those who need it the most. Jesus said as much in Matthew 6:25–33, where he admonished us to rest in the providential care the Creator willingly extends to all he has created. God cares for the poor, and those who would know him must care for the poor as well.

But knowing and doing are two different matters. Most of us would agree that it is a good thing to be helpful to the poor—but acting upon it is something else altogether. When it comes to knowing God, it's the acting in generosity to the poor that makes all the difference. The evidence is overwhelming, almost to the point of being intuitive. Every major religion agrees on this: care for the poor is a necessary step in knowing the Divine.

In my own journey, learning to mimic God by caring for the poor has not always been easy. Along the way, two important lessons have been impressed upon me: *Get help* and *Don't wait.* Perhaps you are like me, and the most forceful lessons are sometimes learned through mistake and failure. The stories I'm about to tell you are about failure but have helped me learn these two valuable lessons. Maybe you, too, can benefit from these two events in my life.

GET HELP

Early in my teaching career I attended a professional conference at which I was scheduled to present a scholarly paper on the prophecy of Amos. I had been doing research on the biblical book of Amos for a number of years and was steeped in the prophet's ethos, particularly in his social sensitivities. The prophet is widely known for soundly denouncing economic practices leading to the abuse of the poorest within the community. A portion of the prophet's message formed the heart of my paper.

The conference took place in downtown Chicago, participants staying in the magnificent hotels near the waterfront. It was an impressive place. I had never even seen buildings of such wealth and beauty, let alone stayed in one. For as long as I can remember, I have always been an early riser, and during the conference I used the early morning hours to walk and view the sights of that magnificent city without the hustle and bustle that would overcome the streets a little later in the day. My travels took me off the beaten path and into some of the poorer, back-alley parts of the downtown region. On one of my walks, I came upon a woman dressed in rags, attempting to keep warm from steam that rose through a sidewalk grate that now served as her bed. As the woman's situation gradually dawned on me, the vast disconnect between my warm and luxurious hotel room and the grate upon which this woman slept hit me hard. I couldn't shake the words of Amos, warning me about trampling "the head of the poor into the dust of the earth" (Amos 2:7). I had to do something, and so I approached the woman with a handful of money, my spending money for the conference, intending to give it to her so she could buy a meal and perhaps afford a warmer place to stay for a night or two. But despite my reassuring words and offer of money, the nearer I approached the more her panic grew until finally she screamed and bolted, running down the street and around the corner. I stood there dumbfounded for a moment and then began to cry. I had failed, and my failure hit me just as if I had been clubbed with a rod. Here I was, pretending to be an expert in one of the most socially conscious of all the Hebrew prophets, preparing to present a learned paper on the document bearing his name, and I could not even find a way to buy an old lady a cup of hot coffee. My expertise in Amos now witnessed against me.

Despite my years of preparation, having read the prophet over and over and familiarizing myself with everything that's ever been written about the prophecy, I was unable to act upon the simplest of the prophet's directives. The terror in that woman's face and the shrillness in her scream gave ample testimony to years of abuse and fright. Her suffering was not her doing and my feelings of self-pity and remorse did her no good at all. How could God be in this? If I was to be effective at all in my care for those who need it the most, I needed help.

Don't Wait

A second lesson followed hard on the heels of the first.

Years ago I spent a number of weeks in eastern Africa. It was a difficult time for people in that region as the devastating consequences of drought became compounded with the horrors of war. The city in which I was staying changed hands as the governmental force fled, and the city was overrun by an occupying rebel force. A dusk-to-dawn curfew was put in effect with violators shot on sight. The frequent report of gunfire throughout the night suggested the curfew was serious but only partially observed. It became my habit to walk the streets of the city whenever I could. Early in the morning, just after first light and right after curfew, I could walk relatively freely. I became familiar with the landscape and the many people living on the streets. On a corner near the beginning of my daily walks was a man afflicted with leprosy and sleeping on a mattress fashioned from cardboard and rags. As the days went by, he eventually came to recognize me and would greet me with a smile and a feeble wave as I walked past his street corner. We never spoke. A wave was the extent of our exchange. I was simply the strange white foreigner walking by every morning. We never spoke.

As the date for my departure and return to my home in the West drew near, I determined to share with this man some of the wealth I took for granted. I knew it was highly unlikely I would be returning to this place anytime soon and it was not possible for me to take currency out of country, so I decided to give away all the money I had accumulated during my stay. On my last morning walk I approached the corner, money bulging in my pockets and feeling quite satisfied with the gesture of kindness I was about to perform. But as I neared the man's rag mattress, it was easy to see that something was desperately wrong. He had died in the night and the courtiers of death, the flies and the dogs, had already gathered. I was too late. The money filling my pockets, only moments before a self-conceived gesture of my kindness, now became ample evidence of my cold selfishness and self-righteousness.

I could easily have shared the money with this man a week or a month earlier. I could easily have brought to him a cup of soup or a bottle of clean water on my daily walks (Matthew 25:31–46 haunts me). I could have learned his name. But in that moment, as I stood next to his lifeless body, with money in hand, I had no excuse and my own poverty was all too evident. I never learned his name. We never spoke.

GET HELP, DON'T WAIT

These two events have burned their way into my memory so that I can remember fine details from each as if they occurred only yesterday. Despite whatever good intentions I may have had, my clumsiness and procrastination prevented me from living out what I knew to be right. And someone else paid a terrible price for my mistakes. These two unnamed, dirty, and helpless people have become heroes for me. They helped form my character and taught me lessons I hope never to forget. Now I want to pass those lessons on to you. When it comes to mimicking the character of God by helping the poor, get help and don't wait. The easiest thing in the world is to feel powerless, overwhelmed by the enormity of the need all around us. It is easy to convince yourself to wait until tomorrow or the next day to spend yourself on behalf of someone going without. For those on a quest to know God, neither is an option.

The Hole in the Sky

It is impossible for me to fully describe the conclusion of your search for a hole in the sky. In your own journey with God, there will be places and experiences that are uniquely yours. But this much I can say: Because God cares for the poor, all who know him will care for the poor as well. For some of us, getting to know God will require a change in lifestyle. There's no getting around it. Care for the poor may begin by expanding your comfort zone. You may need to change your normal routine and rub shoulders with people who are different than you. The marginalized and defenseless, the weak and ill, those unable to care for themselves or sustain themselves—these are the people with whom God may be found, and choosing to run with this crowd may well be the most rewarding decision you've ever made. But be prepared to learn. You will receive much more than you give, and you may find that as you help, you actually encounter God in a whole new way.

My Name Is Angel

Before we conclude this chapter, let me tell you one last story. My wife and I were returning home from running a long list of errands on what must have been one of the hottest days of the summer. I was in a hurry, irritable, and more than a little impatient, so I was in no mood when we drove past a scruffy-looking man dressed in a long, dark, and heavy overcoat pushing a bicycle up a long, steep hill near our home. My wife suggested we fetch this man some water from our refrigerator. I knew it was hopeless to argue with her, so with a roll of the eyes and a disgusted "humph!" I drove home to get the water. I insisted she stay in the truck, figuring that if I was going to be sent on yet another errand, she was going to go with me and give up a half hour of her time too. By the time I retrieved the bottles of water and we had driven back to where we had seen this strange man pushing his bicycle, he had walked about a quarter of a mile up the hill. I pulled the truck off the road behind him, jumped out, and ran up to the man, water in hand. I wanted to make this as quick as possible and so simply shoved the bottles toward the man with the heavy overcoat, mumbling something about how much he looked like he could use these. He smiled, took the water, and said thanks. I quickly turned to leave when he shouted after me, "Wait! Don't you want to know my name?" I spun back toward this strange man, but before I could reply he said, "Angel. My name is Angel."

You could have knocked me over with a feather! I was so embarrassed. I learned an important lesson that day. Never pass up a chance to hand out water. "Let brotherly love continue. Do not neglect to show hospitality to strangers, for thereby some have entertained angels unawares" (Hebrews 13:1–2).

Think About It

We've seen already the extent of Jesus' own identification with the sick, unfortunate, and those in prison when he indicated that generosity shown to any of these was actually generosity extended toward him (Matthew 25:31–41). Expect to learn something about God when you give of yourself while aiding those in need. An attitude of expectancy will go a long way toward preventing an unintended air of superiority and condescension when you roll up your sleeves and get involved. Let me conclude this chapter by reviewing two quotes, seen earlier, from Proverbs.

> He who oppresses a poor man insults his
> Maker, but he who is kind to the needy hon-
> ors him. (Proverbs 14:31)
> He who is kind to the poor lends to the Lord,
> and he will repay him for his deed. (Proverbs
> 19:17)

We all do well to think about these statements, slowly and often.

Conclusion: Has it Rubbed Off?

In this book we have engaged in a search for a hole in the sky through which we might pursue knowledge of God. It's now time to test the results. Throughout our journey, we have used three guiding questions by which to assess the validity of statements and beliefs about God: Does it make sense? Is it reliable? Does it work? These three questions are rooted in a firm conviction that our own existence and experience is important and that each of us is inescapably related to a God who is Creator, Redeemer, and Lover. So, in a sense our guiding questions and the God they reveal are in a circular relationship, each leading to the next. But these questions are only the starting point. Thinking about God is not the same as experiencing God or spending time with God. Our gaze skyward will remain incomplete if we seek simply to satisfy our curiosity. We need to go further.

It is altogether reasonable to expect that those who spend time with God should have something of the Divine's character rub off on them. Time spent with God will change us, and a clear measure that determines the value of the time you have spent with this book is by answering a question: Are you any different? If our journey together has in fact allowed a glimpse through a hole in the sky, if we have been able to spend time with God, it ought to show. But if our journey has not changed us, we have not yet encountered the living God. So, as we prepare to bring this part of our journey to a close and go our separate ways, let me ask you: Has anything of the Divine rubbed off on you?

Two of the characteristics that tend to rub off when God is known are concern for the poor and frequent conversation in prayer. As with any friend, talking together and sharing in things she or he loves to do are necessary steps in developing a friendship or personal closeness. Prayer is the way we can talk with our Friend, and acting out concern for those around us is what God loves to do. In the introduction to this book, I explained how as a young child I would lie on my back in a field and search the sky for a hole through which I might see God. I have come to realize that the hole in the sky is not among the clouds. The hole in the sky is found in the quietness of prayer and in acting out concern for the people around me. That is where God may be found, and if we are to know God, we must be found there too.

Early on in this book I admitted that this journey we are on is, in all the important ways, beyond our control. An Unseen Companion travels with us, often leading us in the unexpected and unplanned. If our Companion is, to you, still distant, be patient. The Companion is not capricious. Although we each travel our own roads, and I cannot predict the path that lies ahead for you, I am more convinced now than ever that you are not traveling alone. The Unseen Companion is nearer than you think and in good time will be clearly seen.

Look up. There's a hole in the sky.

Resources

Berger, Peter, and Anton Zijderveld. *In Praise of Doubt: How to Have Convictions Without Becoming a Fanatic.* New York: HarperOne, 2009.

Buber, Martin. *I and Thou.* Translated by Walter Kaufmann. New York: Charles Scribner's Sons, 1970.

Calvin, John. *Institutes of the Christian Religion.* Translated by Ford Lewis Battles. 2 vols. Philadelphia: Westminster, 1960.

Crenshaw, James. *Defending God: Biblical Response to the Problem of Evil.* New York: Oxford University Press, 2005.

Dobson, James. "Dr. Dobson's February Newsletter: America at the Crossroads of History," http://publisher-scorner.nordskogpublishing.com/2009/03/dr-dobsons-february-newsletter-america.html.

Ehrman, Bart. *God's Problem: How the Bible Fails to Answer Our Most Important Question—Why We Suffer.* New York: HarperOne, 2008.

Ham, Ken. *The New Answers Book.* Green Forest, AZ: Masters Books, 2006.

Ham, Ken. *The Lie: Evolution.* Green Forest, AZ: Masters Books, 1987.

Ham, Ken. *The Great Dinosaur Mystery Solved!* Green Forest, AZ: Masters Books, 1998.

Harris, Sam. *The End of Faith: Religion, Terror, and the Future of Reason.* New York: W.W. Norton and Company, 2005.

Harris, Sam. *Letter to a Christian Nation.* New York: Vintage Books, 2008.

Kosmin, Barry, and Ariela Keysar. "American Religious Identification Survey" (ARIS 2008). Hartford: Trinity College, 2009.

Lincoln, Bruce. "On Political Theology, Imperial Ambitions, and Messianic Pretensions." In *Belief and Bloodshed: Religion and Violence Across Time and Tradition,* edited by James Wellman, 211–225. New York: Rowman and Littlefield, 2007.

Meacham, Jon. "The End of Christian America." *Newsweek.* April 13, 2009.

Mills, David. *Atheist Universe: The Thinking Person's Answer to Christian Fundamentalism.* Berkeley: Ulysses Press, 2006.

Morris, Henry, and John Whitcomb. *The Genesis Flood.* Philadelphia: Presbyterian and Reformed Publishing, 1961.

Nietzsche, Friedrich. *Twilight of the Idols and the Anti-Christ: or How to Philosophize with a Hammer.* Translated by R. J. Hollingdale. 1888. Reprint, New York: Penguin Classics, 1990.

Pew Forum on Religion and Public Life. "U.S. Religious Landscape Survey. Religious Affiliation: Diverse and Dynamic." Washington: Pew Research Center, February 2008.

Pew Forum on Religion and Public Life. "Religious Beliefs and Practices: Diverse and Politically Relevant." Washington: Pew Research Center, June 2008.

Pritchard, James. *Ancient Near Eastern Texts Relating to the Old Testament.* 3rd ed. Princeton, NJ: Princeton University Press, 1969.

Sagan, Carl. *Cosmos.* New York: Ballantine Books, 1985.

Strobel, Lee. *The Case for a Creator: A Journalist Investigates Scientific Evidence That Points Toward God.* Grand Rapids, MI: Zondervan, 2004.

Walton, John. *The Lost World of Genesis One.* Downers Grove, IL: IVP, 2009.

Wellman, James Jr. "Is War Normal for American Evangelical Religion?" In *Belief and Bloodshed: Religion and Violence Across Time and Tradition*, edited by James Wellman, 195–210. New York: Rowman and Littlefield, 2007.

CPSIA information can be obtained at www.ICGtesting.com
Printed in the USA
BVOW08s0903090714

358583BV00009B/137/P

9 781456 527365